Alec Wilder
and his friends

Books by Whitney Balliett
    The Sound of Surprise
    Dinosaurs in the Morning
    Such Sweet Thunder
    Super-drummer: A Profile of Buddy Rich
    Ecstasy at the Onion
    John Gordon's Folk Art: A Great Flower-
        ing of Free Spirits
    Alec Wilder and His Friends

Alec Wilder
and his friends

The words and sounds
of Marian McPartland
Mabel Mercer
Marie Marcus
Bobby Hackett
Tony Bennett
Ruby Braff
Bob and Ray
Blossom Dearie
and Alec Wilder

WHITNEY BALLIETT

Illustrated with photographs by Geoffrey James

HOUGHTON MIFFLIN COMPANY BOSTON 1974

All the material in this book appeared originally in
slightly different form in *The New Yorker*.

First Printing   v

Library of Congress Cataloging in Publication Data

Balliett, Whitney.
  Alec Wilder and his friends

  1. Jazz musicians. 2. Wilder, Alec. I. Title
ML385.B24   813'.5'4   74–6272
ISBN 0–395–19398–2

Printed in the United States of America

For Whitney Lyon and Jamie, in hopes they,
too, find their own Sidney Catletts

And, of course, a without-whom
for Charles Bourgeois

Note

The ten portraits that make up this book are of very different people. Three are popular singers (Mabel Mercer, Tony Bennett, and Blossom Dearie); two are jazz trumpeters and/or cornetists (Bobby Hackett and Ruby Braff); two are comedians (Bob Elliott and Ray Goulding); two are jazz pianists (Marian McPartland and Marie Marcus); and one is a songwriter-composer-critic (Alec Wilder). Four of them are New Englanders and two upstate New Yorkers. Two were born in England. One is second-generation Italian and one second-generation Russian. But they share indivisible and fundamental bonds. All are first-rate performers (Wilder included, in his rumbustious Johnsonian way), and all are deeply involved in American music. (Bob and Ray are not excepted; the heart of their work is an ingenious, native improvised verbal music.) They hold a common vision of life that has lately fallen low. They are highly moral people who have guarded their souls, who have, no matter how bad the going, refused to compromise. They have gone without jobs when fashion has turned against them, rather than demean themselves in shoddy ones. They have kept their spirits intact despite neglect, near-privation, and even semi-oblivion. These sterling people, in taking the high road, have bent their energies toward the endless polishing of their arts, and pre-eminence, no matter how tardy or circumscribed, has been their reward. They belong, in short, to that small aristocracy that E. M. Forster wisely delineated in his *Two Cheers for Democracy*. He wrote: "I believe in aristocracy. Not an aristocracy of power, based upon rank and influence, but an aristocracy of the sensitive, the considerate and the plucky. Its members are to be found in all nations and classes, and all through the ages, and there is a secret understanding between them when they meet. They represent the true human tradition, the one permanent victory of our queer race over cruelty and chaos. Thousands of them perish in obscurity, a few are great names. They are sensitive for others as well as for themselves, they are considerate without being fussy, their pluck is not swankiness but the power to endure, and they can take a joke."

But one more bond holds this small aristocracy together — Alec Wilder. He is their unofficial spokesman. The high standards he lives are theirs. The virtues he voices so eloquently they voice in their own timbres and tones. He is their symbolic ringleader, their touchstone. Until he appears, full-length and rampant, in the final chapter, he is everywhere in the book — evaluating, chastising, cheering, listening, talking. Mabel Mercer and Tony Bennett and Blossom Dearie sing his beautiful songs, and Marian McPartland and Marie Marcus and Bobby Hackett and Rudy Braff honor them with embellishments and improvisations. Wilder returns these compliments by urging them on with more beautiful songs. (He cannot write music for Bob and Ray, but his brief summation in their chapter is high and acute praise.) So these ten people form a loose, brave mutual admiration society, a band of amiable, intelligent, gifted people who continually recharge one another's batteries, and who, in so doing, give us endless delight.

Different technical approaches, governed by the situation and subject, have been used in the book. In all cases, though, the subjects' words and voices rightly carry their narratives. There is no New Journalism; Boswell invented modern literary reporting, and we have all been improvising on him ever since.

The beautiful, searching portrait photographs in the book were taken, under various trying circumstances, by Geoffrey James, a thirty-two-year-old English-born friend, writer, trumpeter, and photographer, who took his first important pictures just eight years ago. One was of the late, often-photographed Pee Wee Russell, and it is still nonpareil. James has become a protégé of the great André Kertesz, who should be pleased.

W. B.

Contents

1

The key of D is daffodil yellow

Four scenes from the life of Marian McPartland, the unique and graceful English-born jazz pianist. The first scene takes place early in the spring.

She is seated at a small upright piano in a corner of an elementary-school classroom on Long Island. She has the polished, easy, expectant air that she has when she is about to start a set in a nightclub. Her back is ruler-straight, she is smiling, and her hands rest lightly on the keyboard. And, as always, she is impeccably got up. Her blond hair, shaded by pale grays, is carefully arranged, and she is wearing a faultlessly tailored pants suit. Twenty or so six-year-olds, led into the classroom a few moments before by a pair of teachers, are seated at her feet in a semicircle. She looks at a list of kinds of weather the children have prepared. "All right, dears, what have we here?" she says in a musical English alto. "Did all of you do this?"

There is a gabble of "yes"es.

"Hail, snow, hurricane, cloudy day, rain, twister, fog, wind, the whole lot. Now, I'm going to pick one out and play something, and I want you to tell me what kind of weather I'm playing about." She bends over the keyboard and, dropping her left hand into her lap, constructs floating, gentle, Debussy chords with her right hand. A girl with a budlike face and orange hair shoots a hand directly at her and says, "Rain, gentle rain."

"That's very good. It *is* rain, and gentle rain, too. Now what's this?" She crooks her arms and pads lazily up and down the keyboard on her forearms. She stops and smiles and gazes around the faces. There is a puzzled silence. A boy with porcupine hair and huge eyes raises a hand, falters, and pulls it down with his other hand. "Fog," says the little girl.

Marian McPartland laughs. "That's very close, dear, but it's not *exactly* right." She pads around on the keyboard again. "What's like a blanket on the ground, a big blanket that goes as far as you can see?" The large-eyed boy shoots his hand all the way up. "Snow! Snow! Snow!"

"Right! But what have we now?" Dropping her left hand again, she plays a quick, light, intricate melody in the upper registers. "Twister!" a pie-faced boy shouts. "No, hurricane," a boy next to him says.

"Could you play it again?" one of the teachers asks.

"Well, I'll try." She plays the melody, but it is not the same. It is a delightful improvisation. There are more notes this time, and she plays with greater intensity. "I think it's *wind*," the orange-haired girl says.

"It *is* wind, and wind is what we get when we have one of these." She launches into loud, stabbing chords that rush up and down the keyboard and are broken by descending glissandos. She ends on a crash. "Twister! Twister!" the pie-faced boy cries again.

She shakes her head. "Now, *listen*, listen more closely." Again she improvises on her invention, and before she is finished there are shouts of "Thunder!" "Lightning!" "Twister!"

"I don't think I'd even know what a twister sounds like," she says, laughing. "But the rest of you are very close. Which is it — thunder or lightning?" She plays two flashing glisses. "Lightning!" a tiny, almond-eyed girl yells.

"Very, very good. Now this one is hard, but it's what we have a lot of in the summer." She plays groups of crystalline chords in a medium tempo. It is sunlight. A cloudy day and a breeze and a hurricane follow, and when the children's attention begins to wane, she starts "Raindrops Keep Fallin' on My Head." The children get up and stand around the piano and sing. Two of them lean against her. She finishes one chorus and starts another, and at her behest the children clap in time. She gradually speeds up the tempo until the clapping is continuous and the children, hopping around as if they were on pogo sticks, are roaring with laughter. She finishes with a loose, ringing tremolo. The teachers thank her and sweep the children out of the room. She takes a lipstick out of an enormous handbag and fixes her mouth. Then, in the empty room, she starts noodling a medium-tempo blues. But soon it is all there: the long, tight, flowing single-note lines and the rich, sparring chords; the flawless time; the far-out, searching harmonies; the emotional content, passed so carefully from generation to generation of jazz musicians; and the balancing, smoothing taste. She plays three or four minutes, and then, as a group of ten-year-olds comes billowing through the classroom door, she switches to the Beatles' "Hey Jude."

Marian McPartland lives in an apartment on East Eighty-sixth Street. It is on the seventeenth floor, and it faces south. From the windows of her compact living room, the Empire State and the Chrysler Building and New York Hospital are knee-deep in an endless wash of brownstones. There is a small terrace, with chairs and a couple of boxes of geraniums. A grand piano, which faces away from the view, dominates the living room. Paintings hang on two walls, and the third is covered with photographs, most of which she is in. The business end of the piano is covered with sheet music and musical manuscript, and there are careful stacks of records on the floor below the photographs. She is wearing a flowered top and pants and a big leather belt, and she looks mint-fresh. She makes tea and sits down facing the panorama. She is extremely handsome. Her face, with its long, well-shaped nose, high forehead, wide mouth, and full chin, is classically English. She smiles a great deal and keeps her chin pointed several degrees above the horizon. She has the figure of a well-proportioned twenty-year-old. "I've been teaching four or five years," she says, crossing her legs and taking a sip of tea. "Clem De Rosa, a drummer and the musical director of the Cold Spring Harbor High

School, got me going. I teach about six weeks out in that area every year. I started out doing assemblies with a quartet and then with a trio, but I didn't think we were getting across to the kids. Last year, I went into the classrooms with just a bass player, and this year I'm doing it by myself. I love to work with the little ones — especially the slower ones. I guess it has to do with listening. I'm trying to make them shed their fidgeting and their fears and make them *listen*. Very few of us ever learn how. I think I was first made conscious of it when I was in kindergarten in England and we had a teacher who used to take us on long walks in the woods and fields and make us listen to the birds and the wind and the water lapping in brooks. During the summer, I teach and play at college clinics, and it's terrific fun. Musicians like Clark Terry and Billy Taylor and Gary Burton do a lot of it, too, so there are always wonderful people to play with, to say nothing of the kids themselves. I wish there had been clinics and such when I was growing up. Becoming a jazz musician in those days, with my background and my sex, was like pulling teeth. It just 'wasn't done,' as my father used to say. I was born in Slough, near Windsor. But we moved to Woolwich a few months later, and then to Bromley, Kent, when I was about four. Bromley was much nicer than Woolwich, which resembled Astoria, New York. My family was upper-middle-class and conservative. All my mother's side lived around Slough and Eton and Windsor. My great-uncle sang at St. George's Chapel at Windsor Castle, and my grandmother lived in The Cloisters, on the grounds. Queen Elizabeth knighted another great-uncle, and now he's Sir Cyril. He and Aunt Sylvia came over when I was working in New York at the original Hickory House in the fifties, and they were shocked and mystified by the whole scene. Uncle Cyril took me aside, between sets at the club, and said, 'Margaret' — I was born Margaret Marian Turner — 'Margaret, does your father *know* what you're doing?' My father was a civil engineer who was involved with machine tools. He was an avid gardener, and clever at everything he did. When I was quite little, he made a goldfish pond with all sorts of pretty rocks on the bottom. He let me help him, and it was a great source of pride. I was Daddy's girl, in spite of the fact that I think he would have liked me to be a boy. My mother always used to say to me when she was annoyed, 'You're just like your father, Margaret — pigheaded!' I think they did quite a lot of bickering and carrying on. My mother was rather a critical person, but I suppose it was her upbringing. It was forever 'Do this, do that, pick up behind you, don't be late.' I was harassed by it, and it took me years to grow out of it.

"My schooling was of the times. I started in at a one-room school, where I drew pictures of little houses with snow falling. Then, for less than a year, I went to Avon Cliffe, a private school run by two well-meaning women. I was a frog in the school play, and I was not pleased by that. There was a nursing home, next to the school, where my grandmother spent her last days, and she'd wave to me out of the window every afternoon when I left. After that, I was sent to a convent school. My sister, Joyce — there were just the two of us — was always ailing with bronchitis, and I think my mother enjoyed hovering over her. But I was the strong, healthy ox. Even so, I was scared of some of the nuns. I was hopeless in some subjects, and they were always grabbing me by the neck and locking me in the laundry room. My mother said I'd have to go to boarding school if I didn't shape up. I didn't, so they put me in Stratford House, in a neighboring town. It was a nice school for nice girls from nice families. We had a matron with a starched headdress and we were told when it was our turn to take a bath and we were taught how to make a bed with hospital corners. I couldn't stand the school food or the smell of cooking, and I got sick headaches. But there were good things. I think I learned how to string letters and words and sentences together on paper. And I designed the school emblem — three sweet peas, entwined. It was quite beautiful. And I wrote the school song.

"I had started playing the piano when I was three or four. It was at my great-uncle Harry's, and the keyboard was all yellow. And I remember playing, sitting up high on a stool, at kindergarten with children all gathered around. My mother would make me play for her friends, and while I played they all talked. When I finished, she'd say, 'Oh, that was very nice, dear.' I was angry, but I wouldn't have dared pop out with 'You weren't listening!' I didn't realize that the pattern of my life was already set. I still play while people talk and then applaud. When I was nine, I asked my mother if I could take piano lessons. She said, 'Margaret, you already play the piano very well. I think you should take up the violin.' We went up to London and bought a violin, and I took lessons, but I never enjoyed the instrument. I played in concerts and competitions, but then my teacher died, and that put an end to it. I was studying elocution with Miss Mackie, at Stratford House, around this time, and I had a crush on her. I used to ask my mother if she'd invite her over for tea or dinner. Mummy was a nervous hostess, but finally Miss Mackie came, and it was she who advised my parents to send me up to the Guildhall School of Music, in London. My parents were always saying, 'You better think of what you're going to do after school; we aren't going to keep you forever,' which made me feel like a bit of aging merchandise. I went up to London and played for Sir Landon Ronald, who was the head of the Guildhall, and I got in. I commuted every day from Bromley, and I really worked. I studied composition and theory and piano, and I won a scholarship in composition. I took up violin again, because we students had to have a second instrument, and I studied singing with Carrie Tubb, a retired opera singer. The other day, I came across six pieces I wrote then. They have titles like 'Pas Seul' and 'Rêverie,' and actually they are pretty well put together. But I'd never claim then that anything I'd done was good. The reaction would have been immediate: 'How can you be so immodest, Margaret!' "

The telephone rings, and Marian McPartland talks for a minute. "That was Sam Goody's. They want more of my records. Some women buy fur coats; I have my own record company. It's called Halcyon, and I've put out four albums to date — three with myself and rhythm, and some duets with Teddy Wilson, which turned out surprisingly well. Sherman Fairchild helped me get it going. He died two years ago, and he was a great jazz buff and a friend for twenty years. Bill Weilbacher, who has *his* own label, Master Jazz Recordings, gives me advice, and a small packaging firm handles the distribution and such. A printing of five thousand LPs costs around fifteen hundred dollars. Whatever I make I put right back into the next record. The big companies are impossible, and a lot of musicians have their own labels. Stan Kenton has his, George Shearing has his, Clark Terry has his, and Bobby Hackett has started one. I think this do-it-yourself movement is terribly important, particularly in the area of reissues. What with all the mergers among recording companies, I'm afraid of valuable records being lost. Not long ago, I wrote the company that recorded me at the Hickory House in the fifties and asked if they intended reissuing any of the albums. I think they'd have some value now. But I got the vaguest letter back. So they won't reissue the records, nor will they let me. It's not right. I think that musicians should get together catalogues of everything they've recorded and perhaps form some sort of cooperative for reissuing valuable stuff. Anyway . . ." Marian McPartland laughs, and says she is going to make lunch.

She sets a small table and puts out pumpernickel and a fresh fruit salad. "I was listening to everything indiscriminately at the Guildhall, and I was beginning to learn all sorts of tunes. I have fantastic recall, but I don't know where half the music that is stored in my head has come from. I also started listening to jazz — the Hot Club of France, Duke Ellington's 'Blue Goose,' Sidney Bechet, Teddy Wilson, Bob Zurke, Art Tatum, and the wonderful Alec Wilder octets. I was playing a sort of cocktail piano outside of the classroom, and once, when my piano professor at the Guildhall, a solemn little white-haired man named Orlando Morgan, heard me, he said, 'Don't let me catch you playing that rubbish again.' Well, he never got the chance. One day I sneaked over to the West End, where Billy Mayerl had a studio. He played a lot on the BBC, and he was like Frankie Carle or Eddy Duchin. I played 'Where Are You?' for him, and a little later he asked me to join a piano quartet he was putting together — Billy Mayerl and His Claviers. I was twenty, and I was tremendously excited. The family were horrified, but I said I'd go back to the Guildhall when the tour was over. My father charged up to London to see 'this Billy Mayerl.' He didn't want any daughter of his being preyed on, and he wanted to know what I'd be paid — ten pounds a week, it turned out. So my parents agreed. The quartet included Billy and George Myddelton and Dorothy Carless and myself. She and I were outfitted in glamorous gowns, and we played music-hall stuff. We played variety theaters — a week in each town. We lived in rented digs in somebody's house. If it was 'all in,' it included food. Some of the places were great, and they'd even bring you up a cup of tea in the morning. Meanwhile, my family had moved to Eastbourne. The tour with Billy lasted almost a year, and then I joined Carroll Levis's Discoveries, a vaudeville show, and I was with them until the early years of the war. By this time, my family had given up on me. But my father would catch me on his business trips, and he'd come backstage and wow all the girls in the cast. I was going around with the manager of the show. He was a comedian, and he was also Jewish. My father would take us out to dinner and he would manfully try not to be patronizing. But it was beyond him. He would have liked me to work in a bank or be a teacher, and here I was playing popular music and going around with someone who was not 'top drawer.' I don't think it was real anti-Semitism; you just didn't go around with

Jews and tradespeople. When I was five or six, and my mother
found out that one of my friends was the daughter of a liquor-
store owner, I wasn't allowed to see her anymore."

The phone rings again, and Marian McPartland talks with
animation. "That was my dear friend Alec Wilder. He wanted
to know if I'd done any writing today. He's incessant, but he's
right. For a long time I procrastinated and procrastinated.
I'd start things and let them sit around forever before finishing
them. Alec gave me a set of notebooks, and I jot ideas down
in them in cabs and at the hairdresser. Tony Bennett recorded
my 'Twilight World,' which Johnny Mercer wrote the lyrics
for, and it's just come out on Tony's new LP. Johnny is another
great friend. One evening, he and Ginger, his wife, and his
mother came up here, and Johnny sat right over there by the
piano and sang about fifteen songs. It was a marvelous experience." Marian McPartland clears the table, and sits down
in the living room with a fresh cup of tea.

"In nineteen forty-three, I volunteered for ENSA, which was
the English equivalent of the USO. I traveled all over England
with the same sort of groups I'd been with, and then I switched
to the USO, which paid better and which meant working with
the Americans! Boy, the Americans! The fall of nineteen forty-
four, we were sent to France. We were given fatigues and hel-
mets and mess kits, and we lived in tents and ate in orchards
and jumped into hedgerows when the Germans came over. At
first I played accordion because there weren't any pianos
around. I met Fred Astaire and Dinah Shore and Edward G.
Robinson, and I worked with Astaire in a show that we gave
for Eisenhower. We moved up through Caen, which was all

rubble, and into Belgium, where I met Jimmy McPartland. A jam session was going on in a big tent, and I was playing, and in walked Jimmy and saw me — a female white English musician — and the my-God, what-could-be-worse expression on his face was clear right across the room. But it was a case of propinquity, and in the weeks to come it was Jimmy on cornet and me and a bass player and whatever drummer we could find. We'd go up near the front and play in tents or outside, and it was cold. He annoyed me at first because he almost always had this silly grin on his face, but I found out that it was because he was drinking a great deal. Somewhere along the line he said, 'Let's get married.' I didn't believe him, so one morning I went over to his place very early, when I knew he'd be hung over and close to reality, and asked him if he really meant it, and he said sure and took a drink of armagnac. I guess I was madly in love with him. We were married in February, in Aachen, and we played at our own wedding.

"When we got to New York, early in nineteen forty-six, we went straight to Eddie Condon's, in the Village. I was so excited I couldn't stand it. Jimmy sat in and so did I, even though my left wrist, which I'd broken in a jeep in Germany, was still in a cast. We stayed for a while with Gene Krupa, then we went to Chicago to stay with Jimmy's family. A colonel with our outfit had given the news of my marriage to my parents when he was on leave in England. My father was stiff-upper-lip, but Mummy told me she cried a whole day. I guess my not telling them first was a rotten thing to do, but we were so isolated. You couldn't just pick up a phone at the front and tell them you were going to get married. But when Jimmy finally met them, he charmed them completely. My mother was really crippled with arthritis by then, and he made her laugh, and Jimmy took my father to the movies. They told me, 'He's not like an American. He's so polite.' In Chicago, I became greatest of friends with Jimmy's daughter, Dorothy, who was very beautiful and just fifteen. Jimmy had been married before, and Dorothy had been their only child. Jimmy had sent a lot of money back from Europe, and the first six months in Chicago were spent hanging out and treating people. All anybody seemed to do was drink, including Jimmy, and eventually it got to be one crisis after another. I left him a couple of times, and once I even booked passage on the *Queen Elizabeth.* But it was all done without much thought; I seemed such a brainless person then. And I think I must have been quite awful to Jimmy. One of Mummy's dire predictions was 'If you become a musician, Margaret, you'll marry a musician and live in an attic.' And that's exactly what happened; our first place in Chicago was a furnished room in an attic. But there were a lot of nice times, too. Jimmy and I started working together, and Jimmy was always marvelous in that he was proud of me, he wanted to show me off. We worked with Billie Holiday and Sarah Vaughan and Anita O'Day, and I met Duke Ellington and Count Basie. And we'd go fishing up in Wisconsin and sit there by some lake and cook fish and eat them and watch the sun rise. I had learned all the good old Dixieland tunes from Jimmy, but I was also listening to the new sounds — Charlie Ventura and Lennie Tristano and Charlie Parker.

"Jimmy and I had split up, musically, by the early fifties, and my first gig all by myself in America was at the St. Charles

Hotel, in St. Charles, Illinois, and not long after that I left for New York. I played solo piano at Condon's and then I went into the Embers, with Eddie Safranski on bass and Don Lamond on drums. Coleman Hawkins and Roy Eldridge were brought in as guest stars, and we backed them. I was so nervous I had to write down what I was supposed to say at the close of each set. I played Storyville, in Boston, and then I went into the Hickory House in nineteen fifty-two, and I was there most of the next eight years. The best trio I had was Bill Crow on bass and Joe Morello on drums. Sal Salvador introduced me to Joe one night. He was at the bar, a skinny bean pole in a raincoat, and he looked like a studious young chemist. I asked him to sit in, and I was flabbergasted. I'd never heard anyone play drums like that. When Mousie Alexander, who was with me then, left, Joe joined us, and I was so enamored of his playing that I let him play a lot of solos."

Marian McPartland looks up at the ceiling and laughs. "Whenever I think of Joe, I think of swinging. It was impossible not to swing with him. And whenever I think of swinging, I think metaphorically. Swinging is like being on a tightrope or a roller coaster. It's like walking in space. It's like a soufflé: it rises and rises and rises. The fingers and the mind are welded together. But it's dangerous. You have to leave spaces in your playing. You can't go on like a typewriter. Sometimes I do, though, and I leave no note unplayed. It's hard to say what goes on in your head when you're swinging, when you're really improvising. I do know I see the different keys in colors — the key of D is daffodil yellow, B major is maroon, and B flat is blue. Different musicians spark you into different ideas, which is why I like to play with new people all the time. Especially the younger musicians. They're fearless. Joe used to play enormously complicated rhythmic patterns once in a while and confuse me, and I'd get mad. Now I'd just laugh. Playing with lots and lots of different people is like feeding the computer: what they teach you may not come out right away, but it will eventually. Unless you have a row with someone just before you play, your state of mind doesn't affect you. You can feel gloomy, and it will turn out a marvelous night. Or you can feel beautiful, and it will be a terrible night. When I started out, I had the wish, the need, to compete with men. If somebody said I sounded like a man, I was pleased. But I don't feel that way anymore. I take pride in being a woman. Of course, I have been a leader most of my career, and that helps. I don't feel I've ever been discriminated against job-wise. I have always been paid what I was worth as a musician. So I feel I've been practicing women's lib for years.

"The Hickory House was a good period for Jimmy and me. He was on the wagon and we were both working, and we lived on the West Side. For the first time in my life, I began spending all my waking hours doing things that had to do with just me, and one of them was a big romance that went on, or off and on, for years. But I wanted to keep things together with Jimmy, and we bought a little house out in Merrick, Long Island, and Jimmy's daughter came and lived with us. Joe Morello left in nineteen fifty-six to join Dave Brubeck, and it was terrible, but he had to move on. In nineteen sixty-three, after the Hickory House gig was over and I'd worked at the Strollers Club, in the old East Side music hall called The

Establishment, I went with Benny Goodman. I thought I'd be perfect for Benny, because I had worked so long as a sideman with Jimmy, and of course Jimmy and Benny played together in Chicago as kids. But I had the feeling I wasn't fitting in. Bobby Hackett was in the band, and he'd tell me, 'Marian, don't play such far-out chords behind Benny,' and I'd say, 'Well, why doesn't Benny say something to me?' One night, Benny and I had a couple of drinks, and I told him I knew he wasn't happy with me and to get someone else. All he said was 'Oh really, you don't mind?' and he got John Bunch. So all of a sudden, nothing seemed right — my work, my marriage, my romance. When I got back to New York, I started going to a psychiatrist, and I stayed with him six years. He was tough but very good. He indirectly precipitated a lot of things. The romance finally broke up, and I cried for a week. Jimmy and I got divorced. I didn't really want to do it, and neither did he, but it turned out we were right. Jimmy hasn't had a drink in five years, and I'm twice as productive. We've never lost touch with each other. We still talk on the phone almost every day, and he stops by all the time. In fact, he said he'd come by today."

The doorbell rings, and Marian McPartland jumps up. "Speaking of the devil! That'll be the old man now." Jimmy McPartland comes into the living room at ninety miles an hour, gives her a peck on the cheek, plumps a big attaché case down on the coffee table, takes off his blazer, and sits down. McPartland is sixty-five, but he doesn't look over fifty. His handsome Irish face glows, and he is salty and dapper. He is wearing a striped button-down shirt and a foulard tie and blue checked pants.

He carries his considerable girth the way Sydney Greenstreet did — as a badge rather than a burden. His credentials are all in order — the founder, along with Bud Freeman and Dave Tough and Eddie Condon, of the Chicago school of jazz; the first and foremost of Bix Beiderbecke's admirers ("I like you, kid," Beiderbecke told him. "You sound like me, but you don't copy me"); and a still lyrical and inventive cornetist — and he wears them well. He opens the attaché case. It has a cornet in it, and several hundred photographs. He puts the cornet beside him on the sofa and dumps the pictures on the coffee table. "My God, will you look at these, Marian," he says, in a booming voice. "I found them the other day out at the house, and some of them go back thirty or forty years. There's your father, and there we are, with Sarah Vaughan and Charlie Shavers and Louis Bellson. And here we are on the ship coming over. Look at you in the GI togs and look at me. Thinsville."

She leans over his shoulder and giggles.

"Here we are playing in that pub in Eastbourne when we went to visit your family. And here you are holding a fish we caught in Wisconsin."

"They should be put in a book, Jimmy. They'll just get lost."

McPartland pulls a tape out of the attaché case.

"A guy gave me this on my South African trip, a couple of weeks ago. I'd never heard it before. We made it in England in nineteen forty-nine. You were on piano and you wrote the arrangements. It'll surprise you."

She puts the tape on a machine, and Bix Beiderbecke's "In a Mist" starts. A complex ensemble passage introduces a Jimmy McPartland solo. "Listen to that intro," she says. "How awful."

"It's not, it's not. The clarinet player is out of tune. You know, I don't sound bad. Not bad at all." The tape finishes, and McPartland opens his mouth and points at one of his upper front teeth. "Look at thiff," he says to her through his finger. "The damn toof if moving back. Walking right back into my mouf."

She stares at the tooth, frowns, and straightens up. "You should go to Dr. Whitehorn, Jimmy."

"I don't know. I think I'll have to move my embouchure. I've already started, and it's a bitch of a job — changing an embouchure you've had almost fifty years." He walks over to the window and puts his cornet to his mouth. He makes a little sound halfway between a puff and a grunt, takes the mouthpiece away, makes the sound again, takes the mouthpiece away again, and so on for two or three minutes. The room is silent except for the mysterious little sounds, but suddenly three or four full notes come out. "There. That's better. But it's going to take a hell of a lot more work."

"Jimmy, are we still going out to dinner?"

"Sure, babe. That Brazilian place around the corner you like so much."

"I'll go get dressed."

McPartland goes through his embouchure priming process once more. Then he shuffles through the photographs. "Marian is amazing. There's no one I'd rather be with as a person, as an all-around human being. I have terrific respect for her as a musician and as a person. She's talent personified. Musically, she has that basic classical training, and she's meshed that and her jazz talent. She's just begun to do it

really successfully in the past two or three years. And she's
a great accompanist. She flows with horns and singers like a
conversation. Marian didn't have good time when I first heard
her. Her enthusiasm was overwhelming, and she'd rush the
beat. I'd tell her to go along with the rhythm, to take it easy.
She sounded like Fats Waller, and, in fact, the first tune I ever
heard her play was his 'Honeysuckle Rose.' It was in this tent
in Belgium. I go in and there's a girl playing piano and she
looks English. I thought, God, this is awful. I wouldn't play
with her until I'd had a couple of drinks. I proposed after six
or seven weeks. Real offhand. 'If it doesn't work out,' I'd say,
'you can just go back to England.' She tried to act real GI,
but I could see she was a fine, well-bred person and not a
Chicago juvenile delinquent like me. My father was a boxer
and a musician and a professional baseball player with Anson's
Colts, which were the forerunners of the Chicago Cubs. He
didn't take a drink until he was twenty-one, and then he never
stopped. My brother Dick and I built a reputation as tough
little punks, and we were almost sent to reform school, but my
mother saved us. She was a schoolteacher from Glasgow, and
she knew German and worked as a translator in court for all the
Jewish people. We were hauled up before the judge, but he
knew my mother and told her he'd let us off if she moved us
to another neighborhood, and she did. She was a wonderful
woman, and she always treated me like King James himself.
She had seven sisters, and her name was Jeanne Munn. I'd
go to her father's house every Sunday — his name was Dugald
Munn, and he was an inventor — and I'd get fifteen cents for
listening to him read from the Bible. He had a wee bit of a

brogue, and I couldn't understand a word he said. So visiting Marian's parents was like being in an English movie to me. They were mid-Victorian in style. Her mother was in a wheelchair and very well-dressed and very particular. Everything at a certain time, everything regulated. Tea at four, dinner at eight. If I was late coming back from fishing or golf, Marian's mother would say, 'James, you're late. We've started our tea.' Her father, who was a great engineer, used to knock his brains out in his garden, and I'd help him until the pull of golf or fishing got too strong. He was a nice, conservative gent."

Marian McPartland has been standing for some moments in front of the sofa. She is in a Pucci-type dress and white boots, and she has a fur coat over one arm. "Daddy once slapped my hand for saying 'Blast it!' "

McPartland digs a frayed envelope out from under the photographs and pours out a lot of German currency. "We used to go into people's houses over there and rifle them. That's where all this came from. Some of it is inflation money from after the First War. It was a terrible thing to steal like that, but everybody did it."

"You used to appear with bagfuls of old cobwebby wine bottles."

"I was just well-organized. Once, you needed a piano for a special show, and the colonel gave me the name of this collaborator in the town. I got eight guys together and a truck, and we went to his house and there was a beautiful piano. Brandnew. I told him he'd get paid for it, and we brought it back to the theater."

"I was really impressed," she says. "You said you were going out to find me a new piano and you did. It was one of your finest moments. Let's go and eat, Jimmy."

It is Marian McPartland's opening night at the Café Carlyle. It is her fourth long nightclub gig of the past year, the three others having been at the Cookery, in the Village, and at the Rowntowner Motel, in Rochester. It is in some ways an odd engagement, and it suggests the country mouse's visit to the town mouse. The Café houses, for eight months of the year, the elegant and fashionable supper-club singer and pianist Bobby Short, and it is not the sort of room one associates with jazz; indeed, no out-and-out jazz group has ever played there. By nine-forty-five this evening, when the first set is scheduled to begin, the room is filled, largely with friends and well-wishers. There is a table of business acquaintances, most of whom are amateur musicians. Barney Josephson, the owner of the Cookery, is at ringside with his wife. At the back of the room are Alec Wilder and Jim Maher, the writer. Jimmy McPartland and Clark Terry are at another table, and nearby are Clem De Rosa and pastor John Gensel, of the Lutheran Church. Marian McPartland sits down at the piano, and she is a winsome sight. The room, with its fey, old-fashioned murals and rather dowdy trappings, is out of the late thirties, and she brings it brightly and instantly up to date. In the light, her hair is golden and bouffant, and she is wearing an ensemble that has clearly been thought out to the last fold: a close-fitting cranberry turtleneck, a gold belt, brocaded cranberry and gold palazzo pants, and a gold pocketbook, which she plunks down on the piano. She looks calm and collected, and, smiling slightly to

herself, she goes immediately into a pleasant, warming-up version of "It's a Wonderful World." (Her accompanists are Rusty
Gilder on bass and Joe Corsello on drums.) Despite her out-
ward cool, she sounds jumpy. Her chords blare a little, an
arpeggio stumbles, her time is a second or two off. In the next
number, a long, medium-tempo "Gypsy in My Soul," which
she introduces as a carry-over from the days at the Hickory
House, she begins to relax, and the glories of her style come into
full view. Marian McPartland came of age when pianistic
giants roamed the earth — Earl Hines, Fats Waller, Art Tatum,
Bud Powell — and their footsteps still echo dimly in her work.
But in the past five years she has moved beyond adroit adula-
tion into her own, special realm. It is, in the way of Johnny
Hodges and Sidney Bechet and Tatum, an emotional, romantic,
and highly inventive one. (Her sheer inventiveness is frighten-
ing; her ceaseless ideas sometimes trample one another.) Her
slow ballads suggest rain forests. The chords are massed and
dark and overhanging, the harmonies thick and new and almost impenetrable. And her slow blues are much the same:
the tremolos are mountainous, the arpeggios cascades, the blue
notes heavy and keening. But her slow blues also have a
singular Celtic bagpipe quality. Her foliage is thinner at faster
tempos. There are pauses between the stunning, whipping
single-note melodic lines, and her chords, often played off beat,
are used as recharging way stations. Her notes have room to
breathe, and her chordal passages are copses rather than
jungles. "Gypsy in My Soul" is sumptuous and crowded, and
so is the theme from "Summer of '42." But then she moves
lightly and swiftly through medium-fast renditions of "All the

Things You Are," part of which is translated into contrapuntal, Bach-like lines, and "Stompin' at the Savoy," which is full of laughing, winding arpeggios. The room is swaying and rocking, and before it can subside she drops abruptly into a delicate, veiled ad-lib reading of "Little Girl Blue." It is a hymn, a lullaby, a crooning. A bushy, luxuriant slow blues goes by, and then she pays Alec Wilder tribute with a gentle blending of his three best-known tunes — "I'll Be Around," "While We're Young," and "It's So Peaceful in the Country." They are fresh, mindful versions, and Wilder, listening intently, looks pleased. She closes the set with a rambunctious, homestretch "Royal Garden Blues," and after the applause, which is long and cheerful, she stops briefly at Wilder's table. He asks her how she feels. "I was flipping at first," she replies. "But then the marvelous vibes from all these dear people got to me, and it began to feel very good. Very, *very* good, in fact. I think it's going to be a nice date."

2

A queenly aura

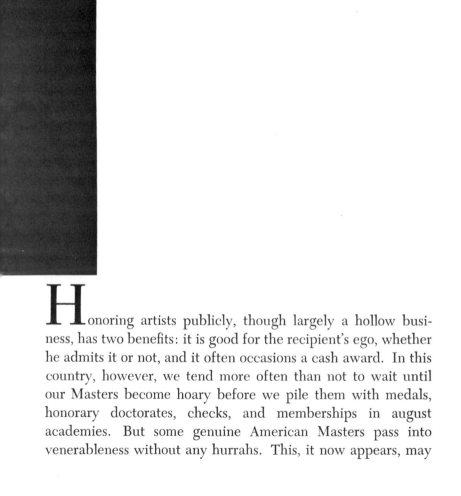

Honoring artists publicly, though largely a hollow business, has two benefits: it is good for the recipient's ego, whether he admits it or not, and it often occasions a cash award. In this country, however, we tend more often than not to wait until our Masters become hoary before we pile them with medals, honorary doctorates, checks, and memberships in august academies. But some genuine American Masters pass into venerableness without any hurrahs. This, it now appears, may be the plight of Mabel Mercer, who remains the matchless but largely unknown *doyenne* of American popular singing. Since 1941, when she settled in this country, she has been the god-head of her art, and at her feet, in rapt study, have sat such disparate admirers as Frank Sinatra, Billie Holiday, Leontyne Price, Bobby Short, Ethel Merman, Eileen Farrell, and Roberta Flack, not to mention Blossom Dearie, Tony Bennett, Mel Tormé, Margaret Whiting, Nat Cole, Peggy Lee, and Lena Horne. (Sinatra has said, without hyperbole, that Mabel Mercer taught him everything he knows.) At the same time, she has spurred on countless songwriters — by causing them to write some of their best songs for her (Alec Wilder's "It's So Peaceful in the Country" and Bart Howard's "Would You Believe It," to name but two), by rescuing their songs from oblivion (such as the Rodgers and Hart "Little Girl Blue," done in 1935 for the musical *Jumbo* and forgotten soon after), or by giving their songs interpretations that are simply perfect (Cole Porter considered her rendition of his "Just One of Those Things" the finest he ever heard). Wilder, who is quick to damn and slow to praise, has set down his thoughts about Mabel Mercer: "She transmutes popular song to the extent that by means of her taste, phrasing, and intensity it becomes an integral part of legitimate music. When she sings a song, it is instantly ageless. It might have been composed the day before, but, once given the musical dignity of her interpreta-tion, it is no longer a swatch of this season's fashion but a permanent part of vocal literature. She has never made the slightest attempt to sing in the manner one expects of popular singers. As a result, those who assume that a 'swinging' style is a prerequisite of a singer of such songs are sometimes thrown off or baffled by her constant dignification (if I may risk such a word) of otherwise casual songs. It is not that she is unaware of the rhythmic looseness of an up-tempo song or of a slow blues. It is rather that her purpose is to present a musical point of view which has more to do with the intimate concert hall than with a casual night spot. That impalpable quality known as showmanship is, in her case, inapplicable. Rather she exhibits graciousness, magnetism, profound calm, and, most of all, complete authority."

More by accident than by design, Mabel Mercer has spent most of her career singing in supper clubs, and so she is, in the best sense, a miniaturist, who sings to small audiences in small rooms about seemingly small things — a remembered spring, a broken romance, a new lover, a lost childhood. But the supper club — that royal relative of the nightclub — has almost been obliterated by television, and its patrons have dwindled and grown old. Few of the sort of special, witty, poetic songs Mabel Mercer sings are written anymore, partly because they would seem hopelessly archaic and mannered to Woodstock ears and partly because the insouciant musical theater that bred so many of them no longer exists. Moreover, of all performing artists, singers grow old most quickly, and within the past decade Mabel Mercer's voice has shrunk, and it has become difficult for her to sustain a note with any effect. Instead, she has perfected what Wilder calls a "graceful parlando" — a way of melodiously talking her songs. Her phrasing and choice of tones and insuperable diction — her style, in short — remain not only intact but inspired; it is simply that rests have supplanted the flow of melody between tones. Her singing in her prime was unique. It lay somewhere between the concert hall and jazz. She had a rich, low mezzo-soprano and a considerable range, and her best tones had the elastic, power-in-reserve sound of formal singers. Her phrasing was jazzlike in that she often placed her notes in surprising places and often used jazz timbres. She was able, in an uncanny way, to make her voice encompass not only many moods but their attendant colors — the purples of love, the blues of sorrow, the yellows of humor and good cheer, the black of despondency. She was a superb dramatic singer who could handle with equal ease the *Sturm und Drang* of Kurt Weill's "Trouble Man" and the bittersweet feeling of Wilder's "Did You Ever Cross Over to Sneden's?" Every song she sang seemed to be fashioned out of the fabric of her own experience, and to be an individual offering to each one of her listeners. And she still is a marvelous comic singer, who, by surrounding the right word with silence or by dipping it in a growl, invariably provokes laughter. Above all was her prodigious, easy, alabaster technique — the precise phrasing, the almost elocutionary diction, the faultless dynamics (she never shouted and she never relied on the staginess of the near-whisper), the graceful melodic push, the agile rhythmic sense, and, always, the utter authority.

Mabel Mercer was, and is, just as irresistible visually. Seeing her is not a fleeting experience; it recalls the brief, stunning sequence on television during the mid-fifties in which Queen Elizabeth, in New York, was passing in review of some worthy body. The cameras, on closeup, studied her face as she stopped and spoke to people. She looked drawn and tired, but she was unfailingly gracious and gentle. It was an unforgettably attractive human display. Mabel Mercer has precisely that queenly aura. Indeed, she is now of Victorian proportions — short, quite round, and with fine, luminous eyes and a shy child's smile. Her ramrod posture, swan neck, and high cheekbones make her seem taller than she is. And so do her high forehead, which disappears in a cloud of dark, short hair, and the long, sumptuous, often low-necked gowns she wears. She sings seated in a thronelike armchair, and she invariably wears a bright silk shawl tossed loosely over her shoulders. She is a study in composure. Her chin slightly lifted, her body pitched slightly forward, she keeps her torso motionless and her hands clasped in her lap except when, several times during a song, she describes a series of illustrative arabesques in the air with her right hand or holds it out palm up, as if she sensed a shower. She sings with her eyes half-closed, and she moves her head only to emphasize a phrase or word. (She has not used a microphone until recent years, but, placed casually to one side of her chair, it is unobtrusive.) At the close of each set, she gets up quickly and ducks out of the room. In a minute or two, she resumes her chair and sings two or three encores (she will sometimes sing upward of thirty songs in a sitting), and she is done. Her audiences, released, tend to surface slowly; she recalls times when she has finished singing and there has been no applause at all — presumably because of a surfeit of emotion among her listeners.

When Mabel Mercer came to New York, the city was garlanded with supper clubs, and she worked without pause for twenty years. The fervency of her following was such that between 1941 and 1957 she sang in only two clubs — Tony's and the Byline Room — and when the Byline burned down a new one was immediately built for her. But work has not been plentiful of late. She has appeared at the Café Carlyle and Downstairs at the Upstairs, and she has given a couple of SRO concerts at Town Hall with Bobby Short. Twilights, though, are often the capstone of the day, and for several months Mabel Mercer has been holding forth brilliantly at the St. Regis Room. She is living in the St. Regis during her engagement, and when I called an intermediary to find out if I could visit her there, I was told, a few days later, that she was dubious. She wondered what we would talk about, and she said that there really wasn't much to her life; she had been in show business since she was fourteen, and that was it. Mabel Mercer pursues privacy, she treasures it, she embraces it. Despite constant requests, she refuses to write an autobiography. But after she had conferred with Harry Beard, her manager and amanuensis, she set a day for the meeting. I arrived at the hotel and called her room, but there was no answer, and there was no message at the desk. I turned around, and a short, stocky figure in a brown tweed coat and a long woolen scarf was emerging from the elevator.

"Oh, my," she said, putting a hand up to her mouth. Her voice was low and her accent elegant. "I forgot all about you. I have to go out and pick up a couple of gowns for the Dick Cavett show, which I'm supposed to tape tomorrow. I've done very few TV talk shows, and I'm rather nervous about it."

I asked her if I could go with her.

"Oh, certainly not," she said. "But come to the Cavett show

with me. They're sending a limousine at one. Harry Beard will be with us, and Jimmy Lyon, my accompanist. But while you're here, come and look at the room." She moved slowly through the lobby, rocking slightly from side to side and threading her way between small mountains of luggage. She stopped just short of the King Cole Bar, at a pair of open glass doors. The St. Regis Room seats perhaps seventy-five, and it is posh. The floor is carpeted, the ceiling is blue, and there are love seats and leather chairs and small tables. Mirrors and gold paper cover the walls. To the right of the doors is a tiny, almond-shaped stand, with a grand piano, a microphone, and a French Provincial armchair. The room was full of lunching women.

"It's nice, isn't it?" she asked. She opened her coat and put her hands on her hips. "I do two shows on Tuesdays, Wednesdays, and Thursdays, and three on Fridays and Saturdays. Then I have my two days off, so that I can get up to my house in Chatham, New York, and have a nice rest. They wanted me to start my first show at nine or nine-thirty, and I told them that was too early. Much too early for my people. So I start around ten, and then what did they do at first but close the doors of the room at ten sharp and keep the people waiting outside until the second show began! 'Here, what's this?' I told them. 'You can't do that. These people rush away from their coffee to get here on time and find the doors shut in their faces.' So we've changed all that. They still close the doors, but they bring the latecomers in by a back way. Well, I must go. I'm sorry about today, but you be here at one sharp tomorrow."

I was, and a few minutes later Mabel Mercer came out of the elevator. She was greeted by a tall, stooped man with short gray hair and thick glasses. He was Harry Beard. She was carrying a clothesbag over one arm, and she handed it to Beard. "I've brought two gowns, one black and one white."

"They'll tell you which one they want you to wear, Mabel," he said. "They have their own ideas about these things." He spoke in a concerned, measured way, a nanny clucking over a charge.

A young, good-looking priest rushed up, expectantly smiling.

"Oh, Peter. It's you. How nice," Mabel Mercer said. Peter O'Brien, a Jesuit, spends most of his waking hours shepherding the great jazz pianist Mary Lou Williams. He and Mabel Mercer embraced.

"I just stopped by to give you a cheer and see how you were," he said. "I was moved a week ago to another church, at Eighty-third and Park, but I'll still have plenty of time to be with Mary."

"Park Avenue," Beard said. "Well, Peter, you've moved that much closer to Heaven."

O'Brien laughed, and said he'd stop by one evening next week. A short, thin gray-haired man in a black raincoat and a dinner jacket appeared — Jimmy Lyon. He looked sleepy.

"I'll go and see where the limousine is," Beard said.

"The Cavett people changed the time of the taping from six in the evening to now," Mabel Mercer said. "I told them it's practically impossible for a singer to sing so early. I don't get upstairs from the St. Regis Room until almost three, and I can't just pop out of bed and start performing."

Beard reappeared with the driver. "I put the gowns in the trunk," he said. We all got into the car and headed for Cavett's studio, which is on Fifty-eighth, between Seventh and Broadway.

"I can't very well practice in my room at the hotel, either," Mabel Mercer said. "The neighbors would say, 'What's that crazy woman doing singing in her room?' I did get a reaction like that once in the country, when I was learning a new song. I tried a high note and the cat, Valachi, jumped right up from the floor and landed on my bosom. So now I warm up with a recorder. I breathe through it, and I play higgledy-piggledy music on it. Every night before bed in the country, I go to the head of the cellar stairs and play, and Valachi comes bounding up. In addition to the cat, I always have dogs. Just nondescript dogs that come and go. I love animals. Deer come within a hundred feet of the house and stand there with their heads in the air. And there are foxes and raccoons. I have some neighbors who had a bunch of raccoons last summer who'd come to their screen door in the kitchen every evening after dinner and pry it open and then let it bang. They'd keep doing it until they were fed with graham crackers and leftovers. You become aware of so many things in the country that city people simply don't know about. Like the crickets chirp-chirp-chirping. To me, they have always sounded like sleigh bells, and it's a pity there aren't more around at Christmastime. One autumn evening a while ago, I was driving by a big field, and it looked totally black, as if some farmer had burned it off. Then a strip of the black suddenly moved up into the air against the evening sky, formed into a flock of birds, and flew away after a lead bird. There was a pause, and a second formation took off, again with a leader. And so it went, a magic, secret ritual. I sat there fifteen minutes watching, until the field was empty. My house is surrounded by cow farms, and I love to see the cows standing on hillsides. I've had the house eighteen or twenty years. My family came from North Wales, and I used to go there for holidays as a child. I remember endless fields of poppies and wheat and blue cornflowers and how we'd return from long walks decked out with bracelets and necklaces of daisies and buttercups, and I knew that one day I had to have a place in the country. Of course, I never could have bought it now. I got it for nothing, and bit by bit through the years, when I've had a few extra dollars, I've fixed it up. I can't garden much anymore, so I'd like to have the place planted with flowering trees — cherry and crab apple and dogwood and wisteria. Then I'd have a thing of glory. I have a huge bird population. I buy sunflower seeds by the fifty-pound bag. The birds take all my pocket money. When I come down in the morning in winter, they're all sitting and waiting on the telegraph line for me to put out some food, and when I do it's as if they were saying, 'All right, boys. The restaurant is open. Let's go.'"

The car pulled up at the stage door, and we all walked to the greenroom, backstage, where Cavett's guests wait their turn. It was furnished with comfortable chairs, a color television set, and fifty or sixty photographs of Cavett's guests in action on his show. Beard helped Mabel Mercer out of her coat. "There goes my stomach," she said. "I've been in this business nearly sixty years, and I still get butterflies at times like this."

"It's the adrenalin working, Mabel," Beard said. He felt the clothesbag. "Uh-oh! The gowns have fallen down in the bottom!"

Mabel Mercer felt the bag. "No, they haven't, Harry. They're folded over hangers. Those are shoes in the bottom."

"I hope you're right," Beard said.

The stage manager took Mabel Mercer onstage, and she sat down in a large yellow armchair. She ran through the two songs she would do — "Too Long at the Fair," by Billy Barnes, and Lerner and Lane's "Wait 'Til We're Sixty-five." They went well. She was told her black gown would be better, and she went off to a dressing room. Beard ordered tea with honey for her. "It's taken seventy-two hours to prepare her for this," he said. "She's like a child who has to go to the hospital. I finally told her if she wasn't careful she'd be all right. But she's so natural and offhanded-seeming she can't go wrong. Mabel has walked alone. She has never deviated from what she knew had to be done. It has never been a question of money or vogue."

Mabel Mercer reappeared, in a resplendent black gown threaded with silver. She had a red shawl around her shoulders. She sat down and sipped her tea. One of Cavett's assistants told her she would be on first and that Cavett would like to talk with her on camera before she sang. The greenroom was filling up. Robert Theobald, an economic analyst, arrived, and then Shirley Temple Black, in a red dress. She sat down near Mabel Mercer and took out a cigarette. "Do you mind if I smoke?" she asked.

"Of course not, dear," Mabel Mercer replied. "It only bothers me when I'm singing. Years ago, in Paris, when anyone started to smoke a cigar in a place where I was working, he would be asked to put it out, and of course he did. It's not that way anymore." A Cavett assistant asked her if she would like more tea, and she said, "Yes. Sweeten the kitty, if you would."

Cavett came in and shook hands with everyone. He left, and the greenroom settled down to watch her on the television set. After Cavett's monologue, Mabel Mercer went onstage. She looked relaxed and elegant, and she spoke easily and with surprising freeness. She told Cavett that her father, whom she had never known, was an American Negro and that her mother was white. She had been born in Staffordshire, in 1900, into a bohemian household full of painters and people in show business. She said that when she was twelve she told her grandmother, who took care of her while her mother was on the road, that she wanted to be an engineer, and was informed that this was not suitable for young ladies. She was put in a convent boarding school when she was seven, and it was there she realized that there was something different about her. Her schoolmates thought that perhaps she was an African princess, but, if she was, why did she speak English so well? In time, she became a sort of mascot at the school, and was given the nickname Golliwog. She said that the only thing that bothered her was that she had short hair and all the other girls had long plaits, so she tied a couple of pieces of string to a headband and let them hang down like pigtails. Cavett asked her about her years in Paris in the twenties and thirties, and she told him about singing at Bricktop's, the famous Paris *boîte*, and about meeting Cole Porter and Vincent Youmans and Gertrude Stein and Ernest Hemingway. But, she said, none of them made a very deep impression, because they were all young together, all struggling together. There came a commercial, and then

Mabel Mercer, seated in the yellow chair, her hands in her lap, her shawl about her shoulders, her composure complete, sang her two songs, with great effect. Her diction was glass, and her voice sure and strong. And she got several good laughs in just the right places in "Wait 'Til We're Sixty-five," a song that has to do with maturing bonds and Social Security and "Tampa, Fla." She came back to the greenroom, somewhat breathless, and there was a heavy round of applause. A stagehand said Cavett would like her onstage for the rest of the show, and she went back. One of Cavett's assistants said that it was the first time she had ever heard applause in the greenroom.

After Mabel Mercer had changed into her street clothes, we all went out through the stage door. It was four o'clock. There was a crowd of autograph seekers on the sidewalk, and she was immediately surrounded. She wrote slowly, but she did sign almost a dozen times. All the while, a huge ABC policeman with a Brendan Behan face and a matching brogue towered over her. He kept saying, "All right, Mabel. You don't have to do so many . . . One more, Mabel, and I'll take you to the car . . . Now, that's it. You'll catch your death."

We all got into the car. "Well, that's the first time that's happened to me in all these years — all those autographs," she said.

"You're a living legend, Mabel," Beard said.

"Don't say that, Harry," she replied. "It makes me very nervous. Let's have some lunch."

"All right," he said, and told the driver to go to Michael's Pub, on East Fifty-fifth Street. It was nearly empty. Mabel

Mercer ordered a Bloody Mary ("I'm going to break my rule and celebrate"), soup, and a spinach salad. "My life has come in three parts — England, France, and America," she said, after she had finished her Bloody Mary. "My mother was short and my stepfather was tall and skinny, and they called their act, which was vaudeville, of course, Ling and Long. I'll never forget one part of it. They'd all put on white tennis clothes and step out on a simulated court and the lights would go down and they'd throw luminous clubs back and forth across the net. My stepfather had invented the luminous clubs, and you'd see these squashy balls of light drifting back and forth through the dark, and it was a beautiful spectacle. In those days, vaudeville was full of jugglers and acrobats and tumblers. The circus is about the only place you find them now. My mother and stepfather had come over to America on tour in nineteen twelve and were stranded by the war, and when I got out of school, in nineteen fourteen, I went into my aunt's act. It was a family singing-and-dancing act, and I started as a dancer. We went all over England on the vaudeville circuit, and we always traveled on Sundays. We'd hire our own railroad coach, and there would be a sign in the window saying who we were. When we'd get to a new town, there'd be the excitement of seeing old friends and of finding out where you'd be on the bill. The closing act was tops, and I think we made it as the next-to-last act a couple of times. In nineteen nineteen, another girl and I formed a dancing act and took it to Brussels, and several years later I joined Lew Leslie's 'Blackbirds,' in London, with Florence Mills. After that, I became part of a vocal trio — two men and myself. We sang everything, a cappella and with piano accompaniment — lieder, Negro spirituals, French songs, 'Yes, We Have No Bananas,' 'Carolina in the Morning.' One of the men had been a choirmaster, and it was he who caused me to start studying singing. I studied in Paris and London, and I had aspirations to be a concert singer. But it just didn't work out that way. I paid for my lessons by working in shows and singing in nightclubs, and that's no way to become a classical singer. I worked in a variety of shows, traveling all over Europe. One was a circus, where we sang between the acts, and another was *The Chocolate Kiddies.* It played in Vienna and in Cairo and Alexandria. I'd go out to the Pyramids every day. It was when they were excavating the Sphinx, and I remember the workers passing pails of sand along and singing chants, like the American gandy dancers. By the thirties, I had settled pretty much into Bricktop's, and it was a lovely era. Bricktop's was very chic, and money was plentiful. There were banquettes around the walls, lit from behind, and an orchestra and a small dance floor. I'd sit right at people's tables and sing to them. That sort of intimate singing is tricky, you know. You can't *look* at the people you are singing to. They get embarrassed. So you look at the ceiling or the far corner of the room, and then they can stare at you and know that you won't look down and catch them. Sometimes we'd sing all night, and once I remember stopping in a café on the way home and listening to Louis Armstrong and Django Reinhardt, the gypsy guitarist, playing duets together. They were still there at noon, playing, just the two of them. In nineteen thirty-eight, I came over here to work in the Ruban Bleu. It was run by Herbert Jacoby, whom I'd worked for in

Paris, and Cy Walter was my accompanist. Then I worked for a while in the Bahamas, where I got to know the Duke and Duchess of Windsor. And in nineteen forty-one I went back in the Ruban Bleu and then opened at Tony's, on Fifty-second Street. Billie Holiday was working across the street, and she came in so much that her boss got mad and told her she wasn't being paid to listen to me."

Mabel Mercer had finished her salad, and she looked tired. She said she was going back to the hotel to take a nap. "I don't remember when I last got eight straight hours of sleep. I suppose it's age. I wake up every couple of hours all night and I read or take a hot bath and sometimes that helps." She patted my hand. "Stop by tonight," she told me.

When I got to the St. Regis Room, at nine-thirty, it was already half full, and Mabel Mercer, again in her black gown, was seated at a corner table with several priests. At ten minutes to ten, she arranged herself in her chair, a green shawl around her shoulders. A wineglass of hot water with honey and lemon and slices of orange in it sat beside her on the piano. She said something to Jimmy Lyon, gazed serenely over the heads of her listeners, and started George Gershwin's " 'S Wonderful." Bart Howard's "My Love Is a Wanderer" came next, and then another Gershwin, "Isn't It a Pity?" After "Season's Greetings," by Rod Warren, she rearranged her shawl around her waist and tied it loosely. Portia Nelson's "Sunday in New York" and Rodgers and Hart's "Falling in Love with Love" were followed by Cy Coleman's "Sweet Talk." Then came Bob Merrill's "Mira," a song from "Sesame Street" written by Joe Raposo

("Bein' Green"), and Jerome Kern's "Remind Me." The Kern was highlighted by beautifully rolled "r"s. She paused for a moment, and then she gave Cole Porter's "Down in the Depths on the Ninetieth Floor" a beautiful rendition, and ended with the songs she had done on the Cavett show. She bowed her way out of the room, and when she came back she did Cy Coleman and Dorothy Fields's "Baby, Dream Your Dream" as an encore.

She sat down with Beard and me and ordered tea and honey. Beard said the Cavett show would be on in twenty minutes, and that he wanted to go and find a television set. I asked her how many songs she knows.

"I guess I know roughly a thousand," she answered. "I can sing three or four hundred of them without too much brushing up. I learned a long time ago that you have to keep your mind exactly on what you're doing when you sing. If stray thoughts suddenly pop into your head, you're apt to forget the words. It's happened to me more than once. When it does, I either repeat what I've just sung or sing a line or two of nonsense until the right words come back. They're always there, stored safely away somewhere in the back of my head. I think constantly about the lyrics and what they mean, and I try and make my listeners feel the vision of what the words are saying. All of us know about sorrow and tears and laughter, so it's not my job to sing *my* emotions but to sing my *listeners'* emotions. Then they can take them home with them. In a way, my singing is like putting on certain sets of clothes every night. I'd be a total wreck if I lived all the emotions I sing about. It happened to me just once. I was sitting at a table with some people and singing 'The Last Time I Saw Paris,' and so many things started going through the back of my mind about Brick's and my little apartment in Paris and so forth that I had to stop and excuse myself. At first, I found this sort of intimate singing a terrible wear and tear. I'd get so nervous my lip would tremble and my legs wobble. I'd pray I could walk across the stage and not let it show. I'd sense unfriendly people in the audience or I'd hear a man leave in the middle of a set and say to the maître d., 'Who told *her* she could sing?' Then I understood that you simply cannot please everybody and that there will always be two or three people out front who understand, and it is to *them* that you should sing. I don't know where my sense of diction came from. Perhaps I got it in school. Perhaps it came from my mother. Before she came over here, she'd take me into an empty theater where she was working, and she'd go up to the top gallery and make me stand down on the stage and sing. I was a very shy child, even with her, but she'd say, 'All right, sing! And I want to understand every word!' "

Beard came back to say that a television set had been put up in the King Cole Bar. The Cavett show started, but there were two Cavetts and two Mabel Mercers, and the colors were a variety of livid blues. Midway in her first song, she made a sound of disgust and stood up. "I can't stand this," she said. "It's bad enough looking at yourself when you can see yourself," and went back to the St. Regis Room by herself. When her segment of the Cavett show had ended, I followed her. She was sitting alone and she looked bemused, and she sighed when I joined her.

"I just don't know," she said. "I've never had any wish to be famous, and I've always wondered: How can those people sit out there and listen to *me?* If I ever have it to do all over again, I'd like to be a painter, like my grandfather. Or a writer. Something permanent. Look at Madame Curie. Maybe I'd write children's books about sitting on the beach and the sunbeams coming down and people coming down the beams and talking to me. Fantasies. But I don't suppose I'll ever have the chance."

3

In the wilderness

The number of jazz musicians in this country who piece out their lives in the shadows and shoals of show business has always been surprising. They play in roadhouses and motel lounges. They play in country inns and small hotels. They appear in seafood restaurants in ocean resorts and in steak houses in suburban shopping centers. They play in band shells on yellow summer evenings. They sit in, gloriously, with famous bands on one-night stands when the third trumpeter fails to show. They play wedding receptions and country-club dances and bar mitzvahs, and they turn up at intense Saturday-night parties given by small-town businessmen who clap them on the back and request "Ain't She Sweet," and then sing along. Occasionally, they venture into the big cities and appear for a week in obscure nightclubs. But more often they take almost permanent gigs in South Orange and Rochester and Albany. There is a spate of reasons for their perennial ghostliness: The spirit may be willing but the flesh weak; their talents, though sure, are small; they may be bound by domineering spouses or ailing mothers; they may abhor traveling; they may be among those rare performers who are sated by the enthusiasms of a small house in a Syracuse bar on a February night. Whatever the reasons, these musicians form a heroic legion. They work long hours in seedy and/or pretentious places for minimum money. They make sporadic recordings on unknown labels. They play for benefits but are refused loans at the bank. They pass their lives pumping up their egos. Some of them sink into sadness and bitterness and dissolution, but by and large they remain a cheerful, hardy, ingenious group who subsist by charitably keeping the music alive in Danville and Worcester and Ish Peming.

One of the most indomitable of these common-grass musicians is Marie Marcus, a Boston-born pianist who has spent most of her forty-year career on Cape Cod and in Miami Beach. She is a household name on the Cape, where she lives. Short, round, talkative, and accessible, she laughs a lot, plays very good Fats Waller-based piano, and keeps her ego alongside her sugar and tea bags. She lives in a tiny gray cottage with blue shutters in a part of Harwich where the houses are within chatting distance of one another and where a Stop & Shop and a Howard Johnson's are around the corner. The house, compact and spotless, has a living room, a kitchen, a bedroom, and a bathroom. The living room looks as if it could be packed up and moved in minutes. It contains a sofa and an armchair, a stereo, a television, a sewing machine, a piano, and a corner wardrobe. The walls are bare except for photographs of her grandchildren and an autographed picture of Oscar Peterson. When a visitor stopped in one afternoon, the front door and both windows were open, and a smart Cape Cod breeze was funneling through. Marie Marcus was on the phone. She was wearing a voluminous housedress, and her blond hair was piled on top of her head. She hung up and perched like a pigeon at one end of the sofa. "That was my mother," she said. Her voice is high, and the edges of her Boston accent have been rubbed smooth. "She's worried because I killed a spider in here last night that looked after I'd sprayed it like it might be a black widow. It probably wasn't, because you don't hear much about black widows on the Cape, but she's all bothered about it. She hates the Cape anyway, and she and my stepfather, Lou Martin, are moving back to Boston next week. He's a fine man, and he plays ragtime. They just celebrated their twenty-fifth, but they're young in action. Then, my mother has always been young-minded. She married my father, whose name was Dougherty, when she was sixteen or seventeen, and she was a live wire, full of pep and energy. She sang in the church choir, and she played piano by ear. And she and my father were great ballroom dancers. They were on the dance floor two or three nights a week at the Totem Pole or Nutting's-on-the-Charles or Loew's State Ballroom. She taught my son Bill, who's a jazz piano player, how to ballroom dance, and he was amazed. He'd never heard of dancing like that. The house where I grew up, in Roxbury — the ghetto is there now — was always full of music, and it was always full of people, too. My mother and father lived in an attic apartment in the house, which was big and old and was owned by my grandmother. She was a fantastic woman who lived to be ninety-three, a woman of the old-fashioned Irish stock, and she ran the roost, which also numbered my uncle and my four aunts. They weren't that much older than I was, and after my grandfather died — I was just three — she raised them all. I was an only child, and for seventeen years I was an only grandchild and an only niece, so in one way I was spoiled. But it was a very religious Catholic household, and those were still the seen-and-not-heard days. So I never seemed to get the kind of affection that my four children give me now. My father was a plumber, and a good one, and he worked at the Charlestown Navy Yard. He was considerate to me and saw to it that I had all the piano lessons and education I needed. But he had a drinking problem that finally drove him and my mother apart. He couldn't help himself, and, of course, there was no AA then. On top of that, drinking was considered a sin, and not a sickness. The poor man died when I was in my late twenties. He was coming home from work on payday, and three men jumped him, and that was it. They never found out who did it. But the music in the house is what's stayed with me. One of my aunts, Mrs. Parnell, would have been a great jazz piano player, but she gave it up when she married. My mother had a player piano and all those rolls by Fats Waller and James P. Johnson, and there were always musicians from Boston in the house. People like Joe Sullivan — not the Chicago jazz pianist Joe Sullivan — who was good in the ragtime style, and Billy Paine, who was a fine singer. It was all an influence on me, and when I was about four I got up on the piano stool and played a whole number. I started lessons, when I was eight or nine, with Miss Teitelbaum, who was a wonderful musician and teacher. We used to kid her about being a nice Jewish lady from Ireland, which she was. I studied with her four years, and when I was thirteen I gave a recital at Judson Hall, in Boston. I continued my music at the New England Conservatory and attended Roxbury Memorial High at the same time. But my career began elsewhere. When I was fourteen or fifteen, I got a job playing piano once a week on a children's radio show, 'Bill Toomey's Stars of Tomorrow.' I accompanied the other kids, and I also had my own solo spot. Then I was hired by Big Brother Bob Emery, who had the most famous children's radio program in New England. He was a strict, smart man and a radio pioneer who'd been on the first Boston station, WGI. I had become a pretty fair tap dancer, and for a while I didn't know whether I wanted to dance or play piano. When I played and danced for a week one summer at a Chinese restaurant in Boston called the Mahjong, I asked the orchestra leader, Jimmy Gallagher, whether he thought I should be a dancer or a pianist, and he told me I had something special on the piano and that there were girl dancers under every stone, and that made up my mind. When I graduated from high school, Bob Emery got a call to do a radio show in New York, and he asked me to go with him. It was nineteen thirty-two, and I was just eighteen. We were supposed to stay at the Royalton, on West Forty-fourth Street, but somehow I got turned around and ended up at the Claridge, which wasn't far away. Emery was in a state of shock when he found me. He told me my mother would have his head, which she would have. So I moved to the Royalton, and I met Robert Benchley, who lived there. He was a friend of Emery's, and he was a delightful man. I had lunch with him several times, and I was fascinated with his witty sayings. I started with Emery at WEAF for Humphrey's Remedies. The show was sort of philosophical, with poetry readings, and I played background music. Then we went over to WNEW, which we helped open, and finally we ended with a children's program on WOR. My mother and father came up from Boston not long after I was in New York, and we took an apartment at the Hildona, over on Forty-fifth Street, between Eighth and Ninth Avenues. I loved the movies, and I went to every show in New York, but I was bored with all the spare time I had. A friend of Emery's owned a bar and grill on Amsterdam Avenue that had a Hawaiian trio, and he hired me as the intermission pianist. After a while, the boss and some of the waiters asked me to go to Tillie's Kitchen, in Harlem. It was a fried-chicken place, and Bob Howard, who sounded just like Fats Waller, was on piano. We went up there quite often, and one night Fats himself came in. I remember the whole room lighted up. He played, and then Howard persuaded me to play, even though I was scared to death. Fats listened, and when I'd finished he pointed to his heart and said, 'For a white gal, you sure got it there.' I was amazed, but I guess he was, too, since practically the only women who were playing jazz then were Mary Lou Williams and Lil Armstrong, and they were still working mainly out West. We got to talking, and I told him that I would like to further my education in jazz and did he know a good teacher? He looked at me and said, 'How about me?' I thought he was putting me on, but he wasn't. He had a small office, with two pianos, in the Brill Building, at sixteen-nineteen Broadway, and during the next year or so, when he wasn't on the road or making records, he'd call me up and say, 'Come on down and let's play some piano.' You couldn't exactly call them lessons. We'd play duets, and then he'd play and have me listen carefully to the things he did. He'd tell me, 'When you're playing jazz, remember the rhythm, remember the rhythm. Make the number of notes count. Tell a story, and get that feeling across to the people. Please the people by making it come from here.' He was very serious when we were working together, and I was grateful for every minute. And I could never get over his reach on the keyboard. He had stubby hands, but he could span way over a tenth, which gave him that great left hand."

Marie Marcus got up and went into the kitchen to get a glass of water. She sat down again and laughed. She is a pretty woman with a prominent nose, a high forehead, and a long face that is balanced on a double chin or two. It is a cheerful New England face, and it is also a child's birthday-party face. "I never make excuses about my weight," she said. "I love to eat, and that's it. But I've been fighting the battle of the bulge for ten years. I have a sign on my icebox door: 'Marie Marcus is a big fat slob,' and one of these days I'm going to pay attention to it. I did try Weight Watchers a while ago. You have to be weighed every time you go, in front of a whole bunch of women, and you get embarrassed. But a couple of jobs came up, and I couldn't fit it in anymore. Now I've started the water diet. Eight glasses a day and just meat and fish. The trouble is I can't stand water. I did take off forty-five pounds in nineteen sixty-nine, but I put it right back on in a year. So I know my health is in jeopardy, and that's a constant elbow in my side. You tend to let yourself go, living alone. My second husband,

Bill Marcus, died seven years ago. He had perfect health, but he had a heart attack and died right on the bandstand. He was a trumpet player, a society-band trumpet player, who worked for Meyer Davis and the Lanins and Ruby Newman. We had just bought the big house next door, and this place — I wouldn't even say what my mother calls it — was the garage. He was a lawyer, graduated from BU, and he had hung out a sign and was starting to practice again, and he had fixed this up as his office, which accounts for the linoleum floor and the paneling. After he passed, I moved in here, and now my three aunts and my uncle live next door. So I use this place for sleeping and eating, and it's all I need." She took a sip of water and made a face.

"My next job was at a speakeasy on Eighth Avenue owned by Dutch Schulz. I worked from ten-thirty till seven in the morning, and then did my radio show late in the afternoon. I was in a little room next to the saloon-type bar, and I was treated beautifully. I built up a following of fans who would come in and scat-sing new phrases they'd heard uptown, where they'd take me on my day off. We'd go to the Savoy Ballroom to hear Chick Webb and Ella Fitzgerald, and it was one of the experiences of my life. Another was being at Benny Goodman's famous opening at the Paramount. I'd heard an early Goodman band in Boston, and something about it told me that this was the coming music. I was at the Paramount for the first show — the ten-o'clock morning show — and I couldn't believe what happened. That music just carried everybody away, and people started dancing in the aisles and on their seats. Somebody grabbed me, and there I was, dancing away like crazy.

The quartet in particular knocked me out, and although I wouldn't wait for St. Peter today, I stayed through three or four shows that morning. From Dutch Schulz's place I moved over to the Venetian Palace, which I think was owned by Frank Costello. It was scary there. Kids were naïve in those days, and I was the most naïve of all. I didn't drink or smoke, and I'd been taught all my life that sex was a dirty word. One night the bosses sent me and this little red-headed singer to play at a private party in a hotel, and when I got there I couldn't find any piano, and I began to realize I was in a strange situation. So I up and said to the hoods who were there, 'If you force me to do anything, it'll be like your kid sister.' They took one look at my Boston Irish face and sent me back to the club. But I never saw the singer again. The Venetian didn't last long, and after a couple of jobs in between I finally made it to Fifty-second Street, to the Swing Club. It was paradise. Stuff Smith and Jonah Jones were working next door, and Art Tatum was across the street, and Billie Holiday was two doors away. I learned and I learned, not so much from piano players as from horn players and singers. It was a fantastic time in New York; there was so much good music.

"In nineteen thirty-seven, I got married the first time. I married a native New York boy named Jack Brown. He was a singer and an m.c., and he ran shows at a couple of Chinese restaurants on Broadway in the Forties. We got a job together at Barkley's, in Brooklyn, and we moved out there. In nineteen thirty-eight, my son Jackie was born, and I had to go back to work two weeks later, because my husband had had a nervous breakdown. He was in a hospital in Brooklyn and then in a sanitarium, where he was for quite a while. Things were never quite the same after that, and eventually we drifted apart and separated, and he died several years later. I raised Jackie, with help from my mother and my aunts, from the time he was fifteen months. I stayed on at Barkley's, and I also worked at the Embassy Club, where I had my own band, and where there were big plans to make a star out of me. But my agent decided I was bushed and that first I should go up to the Coonamessett Club, in Falmouth, on the Cape, where the work would be light and I'd get a rest. It was nineteen forty-two, and the war had just started. I came by train and I got off at Falmouth, and a hostess from the club met me. It was the dead of winter, and I looked around and thought, My God, I'm in the wilderness. But within a week my love affair with the Cape began, and I never did get back to New York. The Coonamessett, which is gone now, was a huge place, with a bowling alley and ballrooms and restaurants, and the work was anything but light. The day after I arrived was St. Patrick's, and the whole of Camp Edwards came over. I was at the Coonamessett or over at Camp Edwards, where I became a sort of mother confessor to the wounded boys, during most of the war. But I was working at the Panama Club, in Hyannis, on V-J Day. It was a high-class steak pub and the number one club on the Cape. It's gone now, too. In fact, I seem to turn most of the places I've worked in up here into parking fields. It was at the Panama Club that I met Bill Marcus, and we were married just after the war. We started going to Florida for the winter, and my two girls, Mary and Barbara, were born there. We worked every winter in Miami Beach and every summer on the Cape until nineteen sixty-one. After that, we stayed up here all year. It was in Miami that I really got deeply into Dixieland for the first time. I joined Preacher Rollo and the Five Saints — Preacher was a drummer named Rollo Layan — and I was with them five or six years, and we were a big hit. We worked every hotel in Miami Beach and had a national radio hookup five days a week and a recording contract with M-G-M. We were on Steve Allen's 'Tonight Show' and the 'Dave Garroway Show' and Arthur Godfrey's program. But it was very hard work. I didn't finish until three or four in the morning, and I had to take several different buses going home and then be up at seven to get the kids off to school. My Dixie experience has continued ever since. In the fifties, I toured the Midwest with Wild Bill Davison, and I worked for George Wein in Boston. I got a hundred and eight dollars and I worked seven nights a week, and when I asked him for a day off he said, 'Fine, but I'll have to dock your pay.' So I quit."

Marie Marcus took a sip of water and made another face. She looked at her hands and flexed them slowly. "I have arthritis. I can't even bend this finger. A doctor fan told me to keep playing and to keep squeezing two little rubber balls he gave me." The telephone rang, and she talked briefly. "That was my friend Mildred. She calls me every day. She lives near here, with her husband, in a great big house that looks over the water and has an Olympic-size indoor swimming pool. I love to swim, and I always have the whole pool to myself. Up and down, up and down, and nobody to bother me. I love golf, too. I was a very good woman golfer. I played in the low eighties when I was at the Coonamessett, and they used to talk to me about going in tournaments. But I've been too busy running all over the Cape and working in every place imaginable. I play full-time summers and maybe two or three nights a week during the off season, when I sometimes do a little teaching to fill in the chinks. Since I've settled here, I've worked the Nauset Inn, in Orleans, which is now the Olde Inn. I played duets there with a wonderful piano player, Leo Grimes, who's at the Ritz in Boston now. He's self-taught, and he told me once that he can't help himself, that he thinks about music twenty-four hours a day — on the street, when he eats, when he dreams, when he gets up in the morning, all the time figuring out new things to play. In nineteen sixty-three, after the Nauset Inn, I formed a partnership with Carl German — he pronounces it 'Germane' — which is still going on. He's a bass player and a singer, and we sing duets. I have a little Bonnie Baker voice, and I sing only with him, because I get very nervous by myself. Carl commutes from Mattapoisett, where he lives, and it's an hour and a half each way. We worked the winter of sixty-three at Mildred's Chowder House, in Hyannis, and the summer in Mashpee, at Ellie's Drift Inn, which is now called On the Rocks. It was the same two places in nineteen sixty-four and nineteen sixty-five, and then we went into the Windjammer Lounge, in Hyannis, where we built up a terrific following. We worked the Windjammer the next four years, with a side job at the Orleans Inn. In nineteen seventy, we were at the Gateway Yacht Club, in West Yarmouth, and at La Coquille, in Dennis, and we did the Lighthouse Inn, the Sandbar, and Deacon's Perch. The winter of nineteen seventy-one, I was with Bobby Hackett at the Gateway, which was a ball, and during the summer Carl and I were at the Hereford House, in Dennisport. And this summer it's the Charcoal Pit, in Chatham."

Marie Marcus looked at her watch. "I'm going over to Mildred's and take a swim, and then I have to get dressed for our Sunday afternoon concert at the Olde Inn. It's with my Dixieland band, which was formed seven years ago. We work eight or nine months of the year, at least once a week, at clubs and private parties and at outdoor concerts. The last outdoor concert we gave it rained, and the electric piano I was playing got wet and I had to stop. Every time I touched the keys I got a shock. Everybody in the band has day jobs, except for Alan Pratt, our drummer, and me. Jim Blackmore, our cornetist, designs heating systems for houses and such all over the Cape, and Paul Nossiter, who plays clarinet and sings and is our m.c., is a teacher at the Sea Pines School, in Brewster. Our trombonist, Charlie Tourjée, teaches at the Dennis-Yarmouth Regional High School, and Jimmy Cullum, the bassist, runs a music store, Musictronics, in Orleans. We hit at four and play until seven-thirty, when I have to get to my regular job."

It was a little after four, and the band was deep in a medium-tempo version of "Pee Wee's Blues." It was set up in a big bay window at one end of a high, raftered room. A dance floor in front of the bandstand was surrounded by tables with red-checked tablecloths. Half the tables were already full. The band finished the blues, moved easily through Louis Armstrong's "Swing That Music," and started the rarely heard verse of "After You've Gone." The band sounded trim and compact and unhurried. Its ensembles revolved slowly and surely, and its solos were brief and to the point. It had a nice sense of dynamics and kept its volume at the conversation level. Blackmore is a gentle, sweet cornet player, cast in the mold of his friend Bobby Hackett, and Tourjée, who is free of the harrumphing approach that afflicts most white Dixieland trombonists, suggests Jack Jenny and even Benny Morton. Nossiter is a fluent clarinetist who favors the chalumeau register. Marie Marcus looked very different now. She was wearing a smart blue overblouse and a long black skirt, and she had vanished into her music. Her mouth moved continually while she played, as if she were spelling out difficult words to herself, and her head went through an endless series of dips, nods, and snaps. Her shoulders rolled, and her feet swung back and forth, back and forth — a little girl sitting on a porch railing and eating a cone. At first, her style seems a simple mélange of chunky chords and brief connective runs, but on closer examination it is a repository of the jazz piano playing of the thirties and forties. In her left hand, she uses Waller oompahs and Teddy Wilson tenths and quick, stabbing Nat Cole punctuations, and her right hand works through short Tatum runs and dense Bob Zurke chords and spacious Jess Stacy intervals. Her melodic lines are short and often affecting, and they duck and bob and weave through complicated chordal patterns that are occasionally lightened by single-note figures. She is a driving pianist, but she never hurries, and her solos have a serene, homey texture, as if she were crocheting them. Her solos meet the listener exactly halfway. She does not bother with dynamics, and she rarely pauses between phrases. The "Satanic Blues" followed

"After You've Gone," gave way to Jelly Roll Morton's "Doctor Jazz," and it was intermission time.

Marie Marcus sat down, dabbed her brow, and ordered a diet Coke. A swarm of admirers appeared, and she was alternately patted, squeezed, kissed, and poked. They included Roland Sears, a sometime drummer, photographer, painter, electronics expert, and disc jockey, who runs a funny weekly jazz program for the Orleans station, WVLC; Heinie Greer, a retired New York lawyer and banjoist, who lives in Dennis and spends most of his evenings faithfully touring the jazz spots on the Cape; Bobby Hackett, who lives in Chatham, and who told Marie Marcus it was high time they made a record together; and Alec Wilder, who had just flown over from Nantucket for a few days' visit. "That felt pretty good," Marie Marcus said. "And I'm in a good mood. The mood I'm in and what I'm thinking about directly affect my music. It's gotten to the point where if I play something in a certain way, people can tell right off what's in my mind. When I do a ballad, I try and interpret the story that the composer gets across in the lyrics. And I'm more melody-conscious than chord-conscious. The melody runs along the back of my mind, and I listen and try to fit pretty chords to it. There are certain tunes I associate with certain people, and when I play them I see their faces before me. They might be old fans who always request that particular tune, or musicians like Bobby Hackett. I'll play 'Memories of You' alone at night in my house and I'll see Bobby in my mind. Playing is always a question of trying to project the right feeling, the feeling of the heart. Sometimes, when you get warmed up, it's a carried-away feeling, and you come up with things that surprise even you — phrases that you *know* you've never played before. This will happen mostly with a good audience — generally a concert audience and not a noisy nightclub crowd. A good audience is like food to me. It sparkles my imagination, and I can run twice as fast. And playing with my band does that, too. I don't like to play alone, the way I am now down at the Charcoal Pit. I don't even have Carl German; the boss let him go, because he said there wasn't enough business. Anyway, the room is big and cold, and I don't feel like anyone when I'm working in there."

Paul Nossiter made a booming announcement to the effect that Bobby Hackett and the clarinetist Joe Muranyi would sit in for the next set, and the band went back to work. There were now a cornet and a trumpet, and Nossiter switched to soprano saxophone. The first tune was a medium version of "Struttin' with Some Barbecue." The dance floor filled up rapidly with middle-aged people whose shapes suggested penguins, giraffes, and hippos, and Marie Marcus was lost from sight for a moment. When the dancers parted, she looked radiant. Her face was shining, her mouth was going, and you could hear her imagination sparkling.

4

More ingredients

Bobby Hackett is a maze of paradoxes. His mood-music recordings, made in the fifties with Jackie Gleason, can be heard daily as piped-in music in supermarkets across the land, but very few people know whom they are hearing. (He is often confused with the comedian Buddy Hackett.) He is possibly the most respected trumpet player in the business, but recently

he has taken jobs where he could find them — playing with a tuba-and-banjo band, with a trio led by a society pianist, and in a club owned by a cousin, to say nothing of intermittent and wearying field trips to Japan, Canada, Italy, and Australia. He is a tiny man (five feet four and a half, a hundred and twenty-five pounds; an admirer recently said he looks like the groom on a wedding cake) who achieves a baronial, walk-in sound. He has been celebrated for years by his adherents as a successor to Bix Beiderbecke, but his passion is Louis Armstrong. Hackett was a rhythm guitarist for two years in Glenn Miller's band, but the most famous solo ever played on a Miller recording is his exquisite twelve-bar statement on cornet in "String of Pearls." His flat hair and narrowed eyes and miniature hawk features give him a furtive twenties appearance, but he is the gentlest and most vulnerable of men. He has been playing for over forty-five years, but he has one of the smallest recorded *œuvres* in jazz. He is the most assured and relaxed-sounding of trumpeters, but he practices a couple of hours every day. And he is a born-and-bred city slicker who lives in the woods on Cape Cod. His style is equally deceptive. He is a lyrical, even emotional performer, yet his solos have an almost mathematical logic. His friend Alec Wilder has said of him: "Hackett is a master of distillation and understatement. For his comment, whatever it may be, is made with the least number of (in his case) notes and each one is essential. He has never fallen into the 'etude' fashion, chasing his tail with neurotic arpeggiations. Nor has he felt the need to flex his musical muscles by means of hysterical high notes. He is both a poet and an essayist. He is never aggressive or noisy; rather is he tender and witty. I have never heard him play a phrase I would prefer otherwise." Hackett plays with sharp rhythmic agility, but he invariably sounds as if he were loafing. His tone is sweet and generous yet unblemished. He is not a great blues player, even though the coloring and feel of the blues are in every solo. When he plays the melody, it sounds verbatim, but close examination of the placement and choice of notes reveals improvisation of the most subtle order. He sounds best when he is playing with stylistic opposites, and some of the most affecting music he has set down has been in the company of Pee Wee Russell and Vic Dickenson and Dizzy Gillespie.

A recent visitor to Chatham found that Hackett looked very different from the last time he had seen him, almost three years before. That was at the annual jazz party given in Colorado by Dick Gibson, the Denver businessman. Hackett had had a couple of drinks at a gathering in Denver the night before the party began. He is a reformed alcoholic and a diabetic, and with the compounding effect of the altitude he fell asleep immediately on the bus to Aspen the next morning, and by the time the bus reached Loveland Pass, which is twelve thousand feet up, his life appeared in danger. He looked like a fish out of water. His mouth was open, his breathing was heavy, and his face was shrunken and gray. Vic Dickenson, who was on the bus and is his great friend, got some food into him when the bus stopped for lunch, and before Aspen was reached he had revived. On the Cape, he looked marvelous. He had a discreet tan, his eyes were bright, and he was full of pep. "You know, this place is something," he said as he went down the stairs to his basement music room. "The air and the quiet and the privacy get to you. I'm up at nine, ten every morning, instead of at one or two in the afternoon, and I feel alive again. I fell in love with the Cape when I first played here, thirty-eight years ago, and I've been aiming at living here ever since. Two years ago, I had a gig all winter in Hyannis, and we did a tremendous business, and that decided it. Hell, when I lived in Queens I spent most of my time trying to make enough money to keep up the mortgage payments, so why not do the same thing in a place like this, where it's beautiful and cheap? So I sold the house down there. Everybody on the Cape is so great. Even in the bank I use. It's run by a lot of ex-show-biz types who give you apples and candy and coffee every time you go in, and then lend you money. Find a bank like that in New York."

A small, dark-haired boy came in and said, "Pop, can you drive me somewhere?"

"Where?"

"Fishing. I want to go fishing."

"Yeh, I'll take you later. Now go find your grandma."

Hackett talks in a deep, soft monotone fretted by a Providence drawl, which falls somewhere between a Brooklyn accent and a South Boston one. "That's my daughter's kid, Bobby. He and his sister, Michelle, spend the summer with Edna, my wife, and me. Their mother works in New York, but my son lives with us. He's a drummer and he gigs around on the Cape. They said it would never last with Edna and me. We met in Providence, where we were both born, when we were ten — at a Halloween party. I even left my ukulele at her house to give me an excuse to go back and see her. Edna's mother was French, and it's funny, I've always had a French thing. I love their music — Ravel, Debussy, Edith Piaf — and I love everything else about them. Edna and I were married in the late thirties. I had just gone to New York and I was working with the Lanins. Lester was taking a group to Nantucket for the summer, and he said I could come if I played slide guitar. I said fine, and borrowed one and learned it. I went to all the trouble because I wanted to get married so bad, and going to Nantucket made it possible. It also made a nice honeymoon."

Hackett put down a trumpet he had been oiling and turned on his stereo system. There were four speakers in the room, and Louis Armstrong's "Jubilee" came booming out. It was followed by "S.O.L. Blues" and "Jeepers Creepers." He turned the volume down. "That's part of a nine-hour tape I put together of Pops' stuff. It has recordings from the twenties to the sixties, and it's all mixed together. I play it all day when I'm here. I can't really feel that bad about his death. I mean, he isn't dead, because we're listening to him right now. And he had a good life. He did everything he wanted and he was worth maybe a couple of mill when he went. I worshiped him. I heard my first Armstrong record in a Providence department store when I was a kid, and it turned me around. The sound has never left me. Later, I got to know him real well, and he was a saint. He was the softest touch in the world. Whenever I went into his dressing room at Basin Street, or someplace like that, it would be full of broken-down musicians and show-biz types looking for a buck. It finally got so that Joe Glaser, who managed Pops most of his life, put a twenty-dollar lid on each handout. Even so, I think he helped support hundreds of people. It was one of his greatest pleasures. He always made you feel relaxed, made you feel at home. Probably because his philosophy about life was, Man, it's all in fun. In fact, he told me once — that voice way down there in his shoes — 'It's a good thing Joe Glaser don't know it, but I'd do all this for nothing.' I'd visit him in Queens whenever we were both in town. Once, he was playing at Freedomland, and I met him there when he was finished. We went to his house and he got into his Bermuda shorts. Then we went to some nightclub nearby, and walking in with Pops was like walking in with God. We went to a Mrs. Davenport's house in Astoria after, and we ate. She had a Hammond organ, and Pops sat down and played for a good half hour, just ad-libbing and composing little things to himself. I think it was the musical highlight of my life. We went back to his house and we wound up in his bedroom, with him on the bed in his underwear and me sitting in a chair, and we talked about trumpet players. He always said good, nice things about other horn players, like 'Sweets Edison should take that mute out,' but you had to read him close sometimes, because he'd get names and words all mixed up. Al Hirt always came out 'Milt Hoit,' after the organist Milt Herth, and he always called George Wein 'Ted Weems.' What tickled me was when somebody pressed him real hard once about saying who was better — Billy Butterfield or me — he thought a while and finally said, 'Bobby. He got more ingredients.' "

Hackett is a chain smoker, and he paused and lit another cigarette. "I'm going to get some coffee." He turned the Armstrong tape up again, and "Bye and Bye" came on. The room was cool and dark and comfortable. The shades were drawn — an occupational badge in musicians' houses. Hackett's stereo equipment was laid out on floor-to-ceiling shelves against one wall, and there was a piano against another wall. On the two other walls were an abstract oil, done in 1961 by Pee Wee Russell; an affecting photograph of Hackett seated outdoors and looking down at a trumpet he is holding between his knees; and two photographs of Armstrong. In one, he is standing in a room in his house beside a row of Eskys — Oscar-like statuettes awarded each year in the forties to poll-winning musicians by *Esquire*. The picture is signed "Best Wishes to 'Bobby.' They Don't Come Any Finer — Louis Satchmo." In the other, Armstrong stands beside Hackett and has an arm draped around his shoulders. Hackett is dressed in a rakish trenchcoat and is smiling brilliantly. The "West End Blues" started, and Hackett reappeared with his coffee. He dragged the piano bench over and put the cup on it. Then he turned down the music again and lit another cigarette.

"Pops taught me so much. Once, on one of those Timex television shows, I was supposed to play a solo between his vocal and Jack Teagarden's. It was a slow, slow number, and the first time I tried it I just stumbled. He leaned over to me and said, 'Play whole notes, Bobby, play whole notes.' And, of course, he was right. And the reason I've finally switched from cornet to trumpet is that he was after me to do it for years. He kept saying that if the cornet was all that good everybody would play it. Right again. He also taught me by his example that the key to music, the key to life, is concentration. When I solo, I listen to the piano and the other instruments, and I try to play against what they're doing. But the ideal way to play would be to concentrate to such an extent that all you could hear was yourself, which is something I have been trying to do all my life, to make my music absolutely pure. You either hit home runs or you strike out in this business. Anything in between, you're second-rate. The tune itself has a good deal to do with the way I play. If it's a good tune, I don't change the composer's lines. Any player who edits Ellington or Gershwin or Fats Waller implies that he knows more. The challenge in an Ellington tune is to see what you can do to embellish it. But to tamper with the harmony is like altering a great architect's work. I respect harmonic law and I live within that law. The best way to think when you solo — I learned this from Vic Dickenson — is in subdivisions of four, like four bars at a time. And, of course, all good players play rubato. Your tempo has to be firm, but you are flexible within that. You rob notes here and put them there, and you rob notes there and put them here. The hardest thing of all is to play straight melody and make it sound like you. It's stripping the medium down to its bare parts. I try and practice two or three hours a day, and when I do I feel right when I play that night. And I've studied — with Ernest Williams, a great trumpet teacher in Brooklyn, and with Benny Baker, who's worked with ninety per cent of the trumpet players in New York. You've got to learn the underneath before you can do the top, just as you can't start school in the ninth grade. One of the most important things I learned, though, was from Glenn Miller. He showed me that most jazz musicians have everything backward. They tend to play two beats to the bar at slow tempos when they should play four beats, which would close up all those holes, and they play four beats at fast tempos when they should play two, which would make things sound less cluttered."

Hackett crumpled up an empty cigarette pack and wedged it into the ashtray, which was a midget version of the standing ashtrays that used to populate hotel lobbies. He opened a new pack and took out a cigarette and lit it. "Miller hired me as a rhythm guitarist in nineteen forty-one. He made me get an electric guitar, which very few people played then, and I carried that amplifier all over the United States, but I never plugged it in. He was a brilliant man, an honorable man. He was a great leader, with a fantastic sense of programming. When a band sounds the same all the time, it's like wearing white on white. And he was a genius for editing arrangements. He'd listen to a new one and he'd suggest a slightly different voicing or a different tempo or a different background behind a solo, and the whole thing would suddenly fall into place. Like 'Chattanooga Choo-Choo,' which was a million-seller. I was with the band when the picture *Orchestra Wives* was made. Ernie Caceres, who played baritone saxophone and clarinet with the band, was my buddy, and we'd be out until five or six every morning, and we'd be a wreck when we got to the studio at eight. So we persuaded Lucien Ballard, who was the head cameraman, to let us sit at either end of the band, where we'd be out of camera range and could doze. He did, and the only time you can see me in the picture is in a quick pan shot that if you blinked during it you'd miss me completely. Miller's death was a tragedy. The band, of course, goes on and on, and so does the estate, which must be worth millions. It's weird. I was a luxury to him, because he certainly didn't need a guitarist. I think the reason he hired me was that often at the end of shows, late at night, he'd call me down front and we would play duets. He'd play the melody on trombone and I'd work around it on cornet. I think he loved that."

Hackett stood up and stretched. "You wouldn't know it in

here, but it's a beautiful day outside. Let's go up and sit on
the balcony, maybe get a little sun tan." Hackett went up the
stairs and through the living room. A television set was on, and
the draperies were drawn. He opened the draperies and
stepped out through a sliding door and onto a sun deck that
ran around two sides of the house. There were a couple of
beach chairs and a small table on it. Hackett sat down with his
back to the sun. He looked almost transparent in the light.

"After Miller went in the service, I went with NBC for a
year, and then with Glen Gray's Casa Loma band for two years.
I took Red Nichols' place. While I was with the band, I finally
quit drinking. Muggsy Spanier had put me on to AA, and that
helped. I went to Spike, which was Glen Gray's nickname, and
told him I'd be a wreck for a couple of weeks, that I probably
wouldn't even be able to find my mouth with my horn. AA
saved my life. I would have been gone by now. And one thing
that has helped me toe the mark is my diabetes, which was
discovered ten or twelve years ago. I take a shot every day, and
every day it tells me to behave myself. Being an alky hurts in
other ways. I was seriously considered for the sound track of
Young Man with a Horn, with Kirk Douglas, but somebody at
the studio heard I was an alky — even though I hadn't touched
a drop in years — and Harry James got the job. And he was
paid seventy-five grand. I went to ABC from the Casa Loma
band, and I was with them fifteen years. In nineteen fifty-one,
I made the first of the mood-music albums with Jackie Gleason.
I'd met him on the set of *Orchestra Wives*. He was playing
the part of the bass player in the band and working at Slapsie
Maxie's, and nobody had ever heard of him. We had a lot of

laughs together on the set, and it was the damnedest thing, because the last words he said to me were 'We've got to make
some records with you and a lot of strings.' That was in nineteen forty-two. The first album, 'Music for Lovers Only,' cost
Gleason seven or eight thousand dollars, and he had a hell of
a time getting a record company interested. He had a whole
floor at the Park Sheraton at the time, and he was living like
King Farouk. He gave a big party there for all the record-
company boys, and all those geniuses told him he was crazy.
Mitch Miller was with Columbia then, and he said to Jackie,
'Look, I've got all these Harry James things on the shelf and I
can't sell them, so how can I sell Bobby Hackett?' Finally, a
kid who was with Capitol persuaded them to invest a thousand
dollars in the record, and the rest is history. We made six
albums, and all in all I made about thirty or forty thousand.
Gleason has probably cleared a couple of million. I guess
Cozy Cole summed it all up when he said, 'The big ones keep
eating the little ones.' "

Edna Hackett, who is a trim, shy woman with dark hair, appeared with a tray. On it were a plate of toasted peanut-butter-
and-bacon sandwiches and coffee. She told Hackett she had to
do some shopping, and he peeled a twenty off a roll of bills.

"Edna and I have been together one way or another for forty-
seven years. She lived just down the street from me in Providence. I had six sisters and two brothers. There were about
five of them older than me. We were very, very poor. We
moved from house to house. My father was a blacksmith. He
worked for the railroad; he shoed horses. He was an unedu-

cated guy, a wonderful guy, but he couldn't catch up with everything. My mother was a little Irishwoman, and she never went out of the house. She was always there. When I got my first cornet, around twelve, she'd hide it all the time. She couldn't stand the noise. By then I was already playing ukulele and banjo and violin. The first group I played with was a Hawaiian one led by a man named Joe Peterotti. We'd go to his house one night a week to play. And my first regular job was in a six-piece group that played in a Chinese restaurant called the Port Arthur. We played three sessions a day seven days a week, and I made twelve dollars a week. But the spirit was good, and we were on the radio all the time. I quit high school after my first year to take the job, and I must have been fourteen. Joe Lilley played piano in that band, and later he was a choir director for Kate Smith and a musical director at Paramount. The best places to work in Providence in those days were the two ballrooms, the Arcadia and the Rhodes, so I shuffled back and forth between them as a guitarist. I made my first money as a cornetist at the Rhodes. Cab Calloway was playing a one-nighter, and I'd gone down to hear him. He was missing a trumpet player, so they pushed *me* up on the bandstand. I couldn't read or anything, and, boy, the notes went flying by. Claude Jones, the trombonist, was sitting beside me, and he had a pint of gin, which we swigged, and that kept my morale going. At the end of the evening, Cab gave me twenty-five dollars. That was a week's pay then. I put the money on the kitchen table when I got home, and my mother said, 'You got to bring that back to where you stole it.' She couldn't get it in her head that anybody could make that much money in one day. The first gig I had outside of Providence was with a New England band led by Herbie Marsh. It was a winter gig at the Hotel Onondaga, in Syracuse, and two things about it stand out. My ears were puffed up from the cold all winter, and one night after I'd been stumbling all over on the cornet Marsh told me that the hotel manager had told him that if I played one more solo on the cornet the whole band would be fired. Payson Ré, the pianist and society bandleader I played with all last summer, was in the band, and that summer I worked my first job on the Cape with him, at the Megansett Tea Room, in North Falmouth. He encouraged me on the cornet, and gradually I got better. Pee Wee Russell was also in the band, and we did a lot of arranging. He'd sing things to me and I'd write them down, and one of the things we worked out — a 'Muskrat Ramble' — later became a staple in the Jimmy Dorsey book. In the fall, I went to Boston and got my speakeasy training. Pee Wee got me a job at the Crescent Club, which was an upstairs speak. Teddy Roy was on the piano. I used to sit right on the piano and play — guitar and cornet. Some Helen Morgan! I met most of the bad boys in town. I remember one in particular. He was feared. He had six or seven killings under his belt. He took a liking to me, and he'd say, 'Hey, kid. Take care of my girl,' while he went out for an hour and bumped somebody off. Years later, I met him at a hotel in New York where I was playing. He came in with a big group, and one of them was in a monsignor's garb. Near the end of the evening, they all suddenly disappeared. Vanished, the 'monsignor' included. They'd jumped the check, which was seventy or eighty bucks, and I got stuck with it because I was dumb enough to sit down with them. Then I went into the Theatrical Club, in Boston, which was a high-class speak run by Al Taxier. He was sharp and looked like a movie star, and was way ahead of everybody else. We opened the place, and the first week we played regular sets to an absolutely empty house. The sound of the music would leak out to the street, and when somebody would try and come in he'd be told the place was all booked up. The word got around about this fantastically popular new place, and the next week they started letting people in. They grossed a million dollars the first year. I guess we had the first real jazz band in Boston. I had Teddy Roy, and Brad Gowans, the valve trombonist, and two sax men, Pat Barbara and Billy Wilds, and the drummer Russ Isaacs. Everybody passing through town sat in — Bunny Berigan, Benny Goodman, Gene Krupa, Murray McEachern, Fats Waller — and the place was always full of Roosevelts and people like that. Fats was a bundle of joy. Wherever he was, everybody was happy. He'd walk into a room and shout, 'The joint is officially jumping!' and that was the truth. He drank a lot of Scotch-and-water, which he always called liquid ham and eggs."

The telephone rang, and Hackett went in to answer it. The sun had moved down behind the trees, and the backyard was full of shadows. It was empty, save for a clothesline, and it dropped off into a deep gully. There were pine trees everywhere, and no other house was visible. Children's voices rang in the woods, and a dog barked twice. A pair of gulls drifted sidewise over the trees, and, way up, sunlight winked on a soundless jet. Hackett came back, grinning from ear to ear.

"That was Vic — Vic Dickenson. I didn't know he was back

in New York. He's still with the World's Greatest Jazzband. He and I had been working together for a year or so when Dick Gibson, who put the World's Greatest together, asked me if he could hire Vic. He was very nice about it, and I knew it would be a great chance for Vic, and better money. So he went, even though he was dead set against it. He didn't want to have to wear his glasses and read music. Benny Morton took Vic's place with me, and when we went to hear Vic, just after he'd joined the band, Benny said, 'He won't have any problems. After three nights, he'll have everything memorized. Vic has ears like a vacuum cleaner.' What I'd like, if I can swing it, is to go into either Dunfey's or the Sheraton-Regal, in Hyannis, this fall with my own group. I'd like to have my son, Ernie, on drums, and Dave McKenna, who lives on the Cape and is the best piano player alive. And a local bass player named Tony DeFazio, who's great. He was a child prodigy, and he tunes pianos now. And do you know what else I'd like to do? One night a week would be open time for people to come and sit in. The Cape is full of people who have been frustrated musicians all their lives — people like Heinie Greer, who plays good banjo, and Monk Morley, who plays alto like Frankie Trumbauer. Music is supposed to be fun, and that's what it would be. No seriousness, no self-consciousness. Just blowing, and to hell with the musicology. And I've got another ace up my sleeve — my own record company. It's called Hyannisport, and it'll be mainly mail-order. Our first release will be stuff we recorded live last winter, with Dave McKenna and my son, Ernie, and me.

"Well, when I was still at the Theatrical, Pee Wee Russell

called me from New York and told me to come down. I'd never been to New York, and I was scared from the moment I got off the train at Grand Central with my guitar and cornet. When I went to the Famous Door, where Pee Wee was playing with Louis Prima, who comes on like a hurricane on the stand, I got so scared I got drunk, and I went back to Boston the next day. But I came back again, and when I did I met Eddie Condon, who was on guitar with Joe Marsala at the Hickory House, and I met the singer Red McKenzie. I replaced Condon with Marsala, and then I went down to Nick's, where I had my first gig as a leader in New York. I think I had Georg Brunis on trombone and Dave Bowman on piano and a New Orleans clarinet player named Bourgeois. Sharkey Bonano had the other band. Nick Rongetti was terrific to work for. People sat in all the time, and after someone Nick had never heard played he'd ask me if the guy was any good. If I said yes, he'd tell me to hire him. At one time, I had twelve guys in the band. Eventually, it worked out that there were four trumpet players there – Chelsea Quealey, Muggsy Spanier, Maxie Kaminsky, and me. Nick would pit us against each other. Whichever one of us was sober, he led the band while the other three were off drunk somewhere. But one night *all* of us ended up in Julius's bar, across the street, and all we could do was sit there and look owl-eyes at each other and say, 'Well, we finally put one over on the old guy.' It was around nineteen forty by this time, and everybody had a big band. Muggsy Spanier had a big band, Fats Waller had a big band, everybody had a big band. So I put one together, too, and it lasted six months, and it was a disaster. I got myself several grand in the hole, and the guy

who got me out, by hiring me as third cornet, was Horace Heidt
— Horace Heidt and his Musical Knights. It was a musical
circus, and I just kept laughing. I was the only guy in the band
allowed to wear a mustache, which I guess was a mark of
respect."

Hackett stood up and flicked his cigarette into the backyard.
"I have to change my clothes. I got a benefit concert tonight
up on the Orleans baseball field with the World's Greatest Jazzband. I think Jim Blackmore will drive me up, since the only
place I know how to get to on the Cape in a car is my bank in
Hyannis. Jim plays cornet when he's not being a plumber. In
fact, he plays one of my cornets. He's a great friend. He says
that when he and his wife, Chloë, first moved to the Cape they
went to sleep every night listening to the Jackie Gleason
records. They've been married twenty-six years, and they
celebrated their twenty-fifth anniversary by going to the
church with their nine kids and getting married again."
Hackett laughed. "So scuffling's the name of the game. But
getting in and out of trouble is where your laughs come from.
So far, I've been able to blow my way out of any situation. But
as you get older you have to get better. I don't believe in
time or age. I feel better now than I did ten years ago. If
you do things right, you defy time. You become fadproof.
The word 'retire' scares me. Once you get as close to a horn
as I have, it's a lifetime proposition. It's a permanent marriage."

5

A quality
that lets you in

As a child of radio and the Victrola, of the microphone and the recording, I have been listening most of my life to American popular singers, and their number and variety are astonishing and almost endless. Their names, which form an American mythology, come easily to mind: Russ Columbo, Whispering Jack Smith, Gene Austin, Jeanette MacDonald, Nelson Eddy, Sophie Tucker, Arthur Tracy, Al Jolson, Kate Smith, Rudy Vallée, Bessie Smith, Fred Astaire, Louis Armstrong, Mildred Bailey, Red McKenzie, Ivie Anderson, Ethel Waters, Bing Crosby, Ella Fitzgerald, Billie Holiday, Tony Martin, Ethel Merman, Johnny Mercer, Jack Teagarden, Dick Haymes, Josh White, Joe Turner, Jimmy Rushing, Mabel Mercer, the Boswell Sisters, the Andrews Sisters, the Mills Brothers, the Ink Spots, the Golden Gate Quartette, Helen Humes, Mary Martin, Ray Nance, Paul Robeson, Maxine Sullivan, Lee Wiley, Bob Eberly, Ray Eberle, Helen O'Connell, Woody Guthrie, Gene Autry, Pete Seeger, Johnny Cash, Eddy Arnold, Noble Sissle, Richard Dyer-Bennet, Helen Ward, Morton Downey, Martha Tilton, Helen Forrest, Frank Sinatra, Georgia Gibbs, Nat King Cole,

Hoagy Carmichael, Anita O'Day, Kenny Baker, June Christy, Eddie Fisher, Frankie Laine, Vaughn Monroe, Frances Langford, Sylvia Syms, Johnny Mathis, Rosemary Clooney, Leadbelly, Judy Garland, Dinah Shore, Billy Eckstine, Eartha Kitt, Buddy Greco, Peggy Lee, Harry Belafonte, Anita Ellis, Bo Diddley, Elvis Presley, Lena Horne, Doris Day, Pearl Bailey, Perry Como, Margaret Whiting, Mel Tormé, Jo Stafford, Tony Bennett, Blossom Dearie, Teddi King, Kay Starr, Patti Page, Carmen McRae, Jackie Cain and Roy Kral, Teresa Brewer, Dean Martin, Sarah Vaughan, Ray Charles, Mahalia Jackson, Bobby Short, Helen Merrill, Stella Brooks, Dinah Washington, Chris Connor, Andy Williams, Steve Lawrence, Eydie Gormé, Dionne Warwick, James Brown, B. B. King, Aretha Franklin, Joan Baez, Barbra Streisand, Bob Dylan, Janis Joplin, Nina Simone, Glen Campbell, and Roberta Flack. They have, in the past forty years, become ubiquitous — on the radio, on records, on jukeboxes, in the movies, on the stage, in nightclubs, on television, and in concert halls. Indeed, they have created, as a huge, ceaselessly moving and changing body of troubadours, the most pervasive and familiar sounds in American life. Many are famous, and some are among the most famous people of this century. Few adults in the western world are unaware of Bing Crosby and Frank Sinatra and Judy Garland and Nat King Cole and Tony Bennett and of the anthem status they have, respectively, given such songs as "White Christmas," "I'll Never Smile Again," "Over the Rainbow," "Nature Boy," and "I Left My Heart in San Francisco." One of the reasons for this unique, engulfing outpouring of song was the invention of the microphone, which, together with its

handmaidens, radio and the recording, made two things possible: omnipresent singing, and a successful singing career without a voice. (Since then, a couple of generations of "microphone" singers have come along. Take away their mikes, and
by and large their voices vanish. Some notable examples:
Blossom Dearie, Mel Tormé, Mildred Bailey, and Chris Connor.) Another was the appearance in the tens and twenties
and thirties of the first great American songwriters, such as
Jerome Kern, Irving Berlin, Richard Rodgers, Harold Arlen,
Cole Porter, and George Gershwin; the lives of their countless
marvelous songs were wholly dependent on being performed,
and so a new and insatiable demand for more and better singers
arose. Still another reason was our old habit of letting off excess
emotional and romantic steam through singing. (Never has
there been more singing in this country than during the De-
pression and the Second World War.) Consider the minstrel
singers, the cowboys, the slaves who first sang blues and
spirituals, the young women who got off the latest Stephen
Foster in the parlor of an evening, the hillbilly singers, the Irish
and Neapolitan tenors, and the light classical singers such as
John McCormack and Lawrence Tibbett. The first microphone
singers were the crooners, who, with their patent-leather baritones and oily vibratos, evolved from the basically European
singing of the McCormacks and Tibbetts in the twenties. And
out of the crooners came Bing Crosby, who, cutting the silver
cord to Europe, almost by himself invented American popular
singing.

American popular singers range from the consummate to the
regrettable. Ella Fitzgerald can do anything with her voice,

while Vaughn Monroe was bathetic. Most of them, though, share certain characteristics. Their voices tend to be home-made and friendly — the kind you feel like squeezing or shaking hands with. Their intonation is often weak and their breathing uncertain. Their phrases sometimes dangle. Their voices, which rarely have much coloration, are a complex mixture of cheerful intent, emotion, electronics, and bravado. But the popular singer's lack of technical aplomb is his great virtue, for it allows him to sing Kern and Porter and Gershwin as no highly trained singer can. Ezio Pinza oversang Richard Rodgers, while Tony Bennett undersings him in such a way that Rodgers' superb melodies seem to come to life on their own. Pinza inflated Rodgers' songs, but Bennett illuminates and aerates them. Bing Crosby was the first popular singer to learn this trick, and he did it in large part by listening to jazz musicians. He listened to Louis Armstrong and Duke Ellington (he recorded "St. Louis Blues" with Ellington in 1932), and he was tutored by Mildred Bailey when he was one of Paul Whiteman's Rhythm Boys. He hung out in Chicago with Bix Beiderbecke and Jimmy McPartland. He learned to sing legato, to phrase in a "lazy" fashion. He learned rubato and the orna-mental, open-glottal notes — the "aaums" and "oowoos" — that made every phrase he sang sound as if it started with a vowel. The great instrumentalists like Beiderbecke "sing" on their horns, and through them he was taught to flow melodically. He learned to make his comfortable, front-porch baritone appear capacious and important. In turn, he taught a generation of popular singers. The best of them was Frank Sinatra. Sinatra had also listened to Armstrong and Mildred Bailey, but he had, as well, grown up on Billie Holiday and Mabel Mercer. (Popular singers such as Billie Holiday are in effect jazz singers, and are more like instrumentalists than vocalists. They use their materials not as harmonic and melodic maps but as departure points for elaborate, hornlike improvisations.) Sinatra was a more serious singer than Crosby, whose offhandedness sometimes gave him an absentminded quality. At the outset of his career, Sinatra sang with Tommy Dorsey's band, and Dorsey, a lyrical player of the first order, taught him — in Dorsey's words — how to "drive a ballad." Sinatra's ballads, freed of Crosby's ornamentation and reverberative effects, took on an almost hymnlike dimension. He *believed* the lyrics he sang, and he delivered them with an intense, clean articulation. His voice was smaller and lighter than Crosby's, but his phrasing and immaculate sense of timing gave it a poise and stature Crosby's lacked. Sinatra, in his turn, brought along another generation of popular singers, and the best of them is Tony Bennett. Indeed, Bennett has become the most widely admired American popular singer. Alec Wilder, who has known Bennett for twenty-five years, recently wrote, "The list of 'believers' isn't very long. But those who are on it are very special people. Among them, certainly, is Tony Bennett. But first I should say what I mean by a believer. He is one whose sights stay high, who makes as few concessions as he can, whose ideals will not permit him to follow false trails or fashions for notoriety's or security's sake, who takes chances, who seeks to convey, by whatever means, his affections and convictions, and who has faith in the power of beauty to survive, no matter how much squalor and ugliness seek to suppress it. I am close enough to him to know that his insistence on maintaining his musical convictions has been far from easy. His effervescent delight in bringing to his audiences the best songs, the best musicians, the best of his singing and showmanship is apparent to anyone who has the good sense to listen to him in person or on records." Wilder went on to ponder Bennett's singing: "There is a quality about it that lets you in. Frank Sinatra's singing mesmerizes you. In fact, it gets so symbolic sometimes that you can't make the relationship with him as a man, even though you may know him. Bennett's professionalism doesn't block you off. It even suggests that maybe you'll see him later at the beer parlor." For all that, Bennett, a ceaseless experimenter, is an elusive singer. He can be a belter who reaches rocking fortissimos. He drives a ballad as intensely and intimately as Sinatra. He can be a lilting, glancing jazz singer. He can be a low-key, searching supper-club performer. (He has gone through visual changes as well. He for a while affected a short haircut and was wont to come onstage with his shirt collar open and his jacket slung carefully over one shoulder. Now, with the disappearance of most of his hair — an occupational hazard that has likewise afflicted Crosby and Sinatra — he wears a variety of stunningly accomplished transformations. He also keeps his jacket on, and is often seen onstage in a necktie.) But Bennett's voice binds all his vocal selves together. It is pitched slightly higher than Sinatra's (it was once a tenor, but it has deepened over the years), and it has a rich, expanding quality that is immediately identifiable. It has a joyous, jubilant quality, a pleased, shouting-within quality. It has, in a modest way, something of the hallelujah strain of Mahalia Jackson.

Bennett lives in controlled splendor in a high, spacious apartment on the upper East Side. At home and on the road, he divides his time between his singing, which is his meat and marrow; tennis, which he took up not long ago and which he believes is essential to his singing well; drawing and painting, which he has practiced, and commendably, off and on since he was in school; and his family, which includes Danny, who is nineteen, and Daegal, who is a year younger (they are, respectively, the guitarist-singer-leader of and the drummer in a rock-blues-country-jazz group); his new wife, Sandy, a cool, pearl blond, pearl skinned beauty from Leesville, Louisiana; and their four-year-old daughter, a jumping bean named Joanna.

Bennett lived some recent days in New York this way:

MORNING

It is a little after nine, and Bennett, dressed in a silk robe, a yellow shirt, and modish tan pants, walks through his living room and into his studio-dining room. The living room, a careful orchestration of sharp whites, oyster whites, and pale grays, contains a sofa, overstuffed chairs, heavy glass-topped tables, a wall-to-wall shag rug, and a grand piano. A bookcase beside the window holds Blake, Picasso, Klimt, Miró, Eisenstaedt, Rodin, Norman Rockwell, Klee, and songbooks by Cole Porter, Jerome Kern, George Gershwin. The studio-dining room is clubbier. Canvases, their faces turned in, are stacked against one wall, and above them, on a cork wall-board, are pinned a map of the United States, the Declaration of Independence, a reproduction of a Bennett cityscape, and a lapel button reading "Quacky Duck" (the name of Danny and Daegal's group). A big, U-shaped cabinet, covered with paints and brushes, is set against the window, and in front of it, on a slab of Lucite, are a stool and an easel. The longest wall in the room is taken up by a white desk and several shelves of stereo and recording equipment, tapes, albums, books, and framed photographs. A small dining-room table and two chairs are in a corner opposite the kitchen door. Both rooms face south, and their windows are enormous; standing in the doorway between the rooms, one can pan easily from the Fifty-ninth Street Bridge to the Jersey shore. The sunlight everywhere looks soft and expensive. Bennett turns on an all-music FM station, then sticks his head in the kitchen and asks his cook, Edith, for a mug of coffee. He takes a bowl of apples and pears from the coffee table in the living room and puts it on a corner of the dining table. A small, new canvas rests on the easel, and after he has squeezed some red, green, and yellow paint onto a palette he starts sketching in the outlines of the fruit. The Beatles' "Yesterday" comes on the radio, and he hums along with it. He works quickly and deftly with his brush, and in a minute or two the outlines of the fruit and bowl are on the canvas. Edith, a trim black woman in a white uniform, puts Bennett's coffee on the desk, and he thanks her. He sketches in a vase of long-stemmed red roses on the table just behind the fruit. "I wish I could stop right there," he says, "and just make it a sketch. I always go too far and clutter everything up. It's just recently that I've regimented myself to paint every day. Painting encloses me in a bubble of warmth. When I'm on the road, I take a sketchbook, and it's a relief, between cities, to sketch everything you see. Later, a lot of those sketches turn into paintings." He puts down his brush and riffles through a sketchbook lying on the desk. There are scenes of trees and houses in Hollywood, of Eddie Fisher's garden, of a rain-soaked park in Leeds, England, and of chimney pots in Glasgow. They are graphic and tight and detailed. "I don't understand why, but painting comes to me much easier in England. It's almost like I slip into a different style." He picks up his brush and points at the reproduction of the cityscape on the cork board. "I'm really pleased about that. It was done right out this window, and the original is in a celebrity art show in Lincoln Center. Red Skelton is in the show, and Kim Novak and Duke Ellington and Henry Fonda. Skelton's painting is of an Emmett Kelly-type clown, which is really a self-portrait. He sold a painting once to Maurice Chevalier, and Chevalier hung it in his house between a Picasso and a Cézanne. Ellington's painting in the show is of Billy Strayhorn, and it's full of flaming blues. It's as mysterious as his music. Henry Fonda's is in the Wyeth school. But I think maybe Kim Novak is the most talented of everybody. She has a beautiful control of paints and a lot of expression. I like Impressionism and the Old Masters — the way Rembrandt could turn out a drawing that was just as fully realized as any painting. I like doing what they did rather than reaching out for something new. I try and paint in their tradition."

Joanna appears in the living-room doorway. She is about two feet high and has long dark blond hair and huge eyes. She is in her underwear and holds a pacifier in one hand.

"Hey, Jo. How are you this morning, darlin'?" Bennett says.

"Fine. I lost my pink umbrella. It was hanging on my tricycle." Her voice is birdlike.

"Well, we'll look into that. Do you want to sit here on the stool and watch Daddy paint?" He hoists her onto the stool, and she looks as if she were sitting in a treetop. She drops her pacifier on the floor, and Bennett picks up an apple from the bowl and hands it to her. She holds it in both hands and takes a tiny bite. He laughs. "That won't make that much difference. I'll just paint it out." He blends the apple into the background and scrapes the results with a palette knife.

"There you are, Joanna," Sandy Bennett says. She is wearing a blue and white patterned dress and a blue blazer. Her hair hangs over one eye. "Come and get dressed. We have to go and get you some shoes, and then I have to get back here and interview some new nurses." She sighs and pouts. Joanna puts down the apple, which has four dime-size bites in it, and shinnies off the stool. "Then I'm going to call the French Lycée, Tony. It might be tough for her, but she can have a tutor, too. There are lycées in Los Angeles and London and Paris, so if we spend three months in any of those places, she'd have a school. I mean, that's what our life style is."

"Right, San," Bennett says, and puts the final strokes on his painting. Joanna runs out of the room and Bennett shouts after her, "Hey, Joanna, do you want to go buy a kite tomorrow morning and fly it in the Park?"

"Yes! Whoopee!" she shrieks, and vanishes around the corner.

AT THE AMALFI

It is late afternoon on the same day, and Bennett is at a back table on the ground floor of the Amalfi, on East Forty-eighth

Street. He has been eating at the Amalfi since the days, twenty and more years ago, when it was a one-room place on West Forty-seventh. Phil Rizzuto, the Yankee sportscaster and former Yankee shortstop, is a couple of tables away, and Bennett greets him and sends a drink to his table. Bennett is to sing a couple of songs at ten o'clock at a benefit, and he has ordered a light supper of macaroni shells stuffed with ricotta and a bottle of Chianti classico. Bennett has the sort of face that is easily sculptured by light. In broad daytime, he tends to look jagged and awkwardly composed: his generous Roman nose booms and his pale green eyes become slits. But the subdued lighting in the Amalfi makes him handsome and compact. His eyes become melancholy and shine darkly, the deep lines that run past his mouth are stoical, and his nose is regal. His voice, though, never changes. It is a singer's voice — soft, slightly hoarse, and always on the verge of sliding into melody. Rizzuto calls over and thanks Bennett for the drink, and Bennett nods and raises his wineglass in Rizzuto's direction. "I'm not that crazy about singing at big benefits," Bennett says, "but Ed Sullivan, who's running this one, has been good to me and I like him. I like concert halls, and what I do now is pick the best halls here and abroad, and give just one concert on Friday night and one on Saturday. I do that about thirty weekends a year. It's much nicer working concert halls than nightclubs. The audience holds on to every inch of intonation and inflection. But nightclubs teach performers like me. They teach you spontaneity. They teach you to keep your sense of humor. They teach you to keep your cool. All of which I needed not long ago when I gave a concert in Buffalo and decided to experiment by not using a microphone. The hall isn't that big and they could hear me, but I guess without the microphone I just didn't sound like *me*. So people started shouting. But I remembered what Ben Webster — the great, late Ben Webster — once told me: 'If I had it to do all over again, I'd leave my anger offstage.' And I did. I went backstage and got a mike, and everything was all right. In addition to my concerts, I do television specials, like the one Lena Horne and I did — just the two of us, no one else — a while back. It got very nice notices, which proves you just don't need all those trappings. I also work in Vegas, and at Bill Harrah's places in Lake Tahoe and Reno, for six weeks a year. Vegas is great, with all the performers on one strip, like a kind of super-Fifty-second Street. They can afford anything, and they treat performers marvelously. But Bill Harrah is fabulous. I think he started out with bingo parlors in Reno thirty-five years ago, and now he owns these big places in Tahoe and Reno and has a huge collection of classic cars. He meets you at the airport with a Rolls-Royce and gives you the keys to the car and a beautiful home with a pool. At the end of the engagement, he throws a party for you in his own home. It's like some kind of fantastic vacation."

Bennett takes a forkful of shells and a sip of wine. "It's beautiful not to compromise in what you sing, and yet I've done business since I had my first record hit for Columbia, in nineteen fifty-one. I've always tried to do the cream of the popular repertoire and yet remain commercial. Hanging out with good songs is the secret. Songs like 'All the Things You Are' and 'East of the Sun' are just the opposite of singing down. And so are these lyrics, which Alec Wilder wrote and sent me a few days ago. He said if I liked them he'd set them to music. I think they're beautiful." Bennett pulled a sheet of onionskin letter paper out of his pocket. The lyrics read:

GIVE ME THAT WARM FEELING

Give me that warm feeling
That makes me believe again,
Give me that soft answer,
The kind you gave me way back when.
Give me some true kindness
That brightens the sky again.
Give me the best that's in you
And encouragement now and then.
Dust off those long-lost manners!
Bury ambition and guile!
Unfurl those lovely banners
Of virtue and laughter and style!
Give me that warm feeling,
Take off that impersonal glove.
Remember, remember, we're dealing
With that fair and that rare thing called love!

"I love singing too much to cheat the public. And I can't ever lose that spirit by listening to the money boys, the Broadway wise guys who used to tell me, 'If you don't sing such-and-such, you'll end up with a classy reputation and no bread in the bank.' But if I lost that spirit, my feeling for music would run right out the window. It's this obsolescence thing in America, where cars are made to break down and songs written to last two weeks. But good songs last forever, and I've come to learn that there's a whole group out there in the audience who's studying that with me. There's a greatness in an audience when it gets perfectly still. It becomes a beautiful tribal contact, a delicate, poetic thing. A great song does that. It also works two ways: the performer makes the song work, and the song inspires the performer.

"All kinds of things go through my head when I'm singing. I think of Joanna a lot. I think of things from my past; I even *see* them. If I'm working in a beautiful place like Festival Hall, in London, I think of the great lighting, the great clusters of light, and they inspire me. If a song is truly believable, it becomes a self-hypnosis thing. And when that happens I automatically start thinking a line ahead, like when I serve at tennis and am already thinking of the next shot. My concentration becomes heavy, so that if I forget the words I can do what Harold Arlen told me: 'Just make up new words in the right spirit and don't let anybody know, and you'll be all right.'

"I've always liked the Billie Holiday tradition of allowing the musicians you're working with to take charge and to solo, and my arrangements are always written that way. Jazz musicians create great warmth and feeling. When they play well, they make *you* sing, too. I've worked with Bobby Hackett and Woody Herman and Duke Ellington and Stan Kenton and Count Basie. And I've worked with Harry Edison and Jimmy Rowles and Tommy Flanagan and Zoot Sims and John Bunch and Billy Exiner. You can't beat the perfection of Basie. He even talks the way he plays: one or two words take care of conversation for the month. Like when he saw the distance he'd have to go to reach his piano on this tiny, miserable stage we were working on somewhere out West. 'Man, that's a long walk,' he said."

Bennett laughs, and tells the waiter, a diminutive carry-over from the old Amalfi, that he doesn't have time for espresso but that he will see him soon. He waves to Rizzuto.

KITING IN THE PARK

It is ten-thirty the next morning, and one of those dancing blue New York days: the shadows have knife edges, and the sidewalks are full of diamonds. Bennett is standing with Joanna at the curb in front of his apartment house. She is holding on to his right index finger, and she barely tops his knees. They are headed for the East Meadow, in Central Park, where a sequence of a quasi-documentary about Bennett's New York life is to be filmed. One sequence has already been done in his apartment, and another will be filmed tomorrow night at a concert he is giving in Alice Tully Hall. Joanna is in a blue knitted jumper with a matching top, and Bennett has on a gleaming white safari suit and a dark olive shirt open at the neck.

"Daddy, let's go see if the flower we planted is still growing," Joanna pipes.

Bennett hunkers beside some shrubs next to the building's door and rubs the dirt with his hand. There is nothing there.

"Whynot? Whynot? Whynot?" Joanna chants.

Bennett looks sheepish. "I guess we forgot to water it, or something. But we'll try again."

A black limousine the length of the one Jelly Roll Morton said he had to take to Central Park to turn around pulls up at the curb, and Bennett and Joanna get in. Bennett rents the car when he is in town. It has a red carpet, and the jump seats are separated by a cabinet containing a bar, a radio, and a tiny television set. Bennett tells his driver, a squat, cheerful man named Caesar, to stop at a shop specializing in kites, at Second Avenue and Eighty-fourth Street. Two cameramen and a grip follow the limousine in a cab. Joanna diddles with the television, switching from channel to channel, and Bennett tells her to slow down or she won't be able to see anything at all. She pays no attention. At the shop, Bennett and one of the cameramen choose a couple of big, semitransparent German kites that look like birds. Bennett is all thumbs, but he manages to get one of the kites assembled by the time the limousine pulls up at Fifth Avenue and Ninety-eight Street. The East Meadow stretches from Ninety-seventh to One-hundred-and-first Street and is vaguely bowl-shaped. Joanna sails in the south gate ahead of Bennett and, sensing the expanse in front of her, takes off up the Meadow, her legs going like a sandpiper's. Bennett, laughing and shouting, catches her at One-hundredth Street. The cameramen station themselves on a low rise on one side of the Meadow. A time follows that recalls the mad footage in *A Hard Day's Night* in which the Beatles race wildly and aimlessly back and forth across an immense field. There is almost no wind, but Bennett gets the kite twelve feet into the air, and he and Joanna run up the Meadow. The kite crashes. Joanna picks it up and runs south, Bennett galloping after her. They go up the Meadow, down the Meadow, across the Meadow. Joanna maintains her speed, but Bennett begins to puff. The cameramen declare that they have enough film, and Bennett laughs and wipes his brow. He picks up his jacket from

the grass and flings it and the kite across one shoulder. Joanna
latches on to his index finger and tows him back to the car.

A LIGHT LUNCH

Before he showers and changes his clothes at the apartment,
Bennett asks Edith to fix a light lunch. Joanna is fed in the
kitchen and packed off for a nap. Bennett is due at three o'clock
at a studio on Christopher Street, where he will rehearse with
the Ruby Braff-George Barnes Quartet. The quartet is to accompany him at Alice Tully Hall. Edith sets the table in the
studio and brings in a chicken salad and a large glass of boysen-
berry juice. "Man, tennis has nothing on that kiteflying," Bennett says. "But all that running around will make me sing
better this afternoon. Maybe if I'd known about it a long time
ago, it would have gotten my career going a lot faster. The way
it was, I didn't become any sort of authoritative singer until I
was twenty-seven. For seven years before that, I scuffled.
After the war, I used the GI Bill to study at the American
Theater Wing, where I worked on bel canto with Peter
D'Andrea. And I studied voice with Miriam Speir. It was at
her place I first met Alec Wilder. I never passed any auditions,
and I worked as an elevator man at the Park Sheraton, in an
uncle's grocery store, as a runner for the AP, and as a singing
waiter out in Astoria, where I was born. I was born in August
of nineteen twenty-six, as Anthony Dominick Benedetto. I'm
using Benedetto again to sign my paintings. We lived in a
little two-story house in Astoria which is still there. My father
came over from Italy in nineteen twenty-two, but I don't know
much about him, because he died when I was nine. He had a

grocery store on Fifty-second Street and Sixth Avenue, where
the CBS Building is now. I remember he was a beautiful man,
who was much loved by his family and friends. He had an
open, warm voice, full of love and melody, and he sang beautifully. He'd always get the family out on Sundays to sing and
dance. My mother, whose maiden name was Surace, was born
down on Mott and Hester Streets, and she lives out in River
Edge, New Jersey. After my father died, she went to work in
the garment district and put my brother and sister and me
through school. She has spirit and that great gift of common
sense. Judy Garland went crazy over her when she met her.
I went to P.S. Seven and Junior High School One-forty-one, out
in Astoria, and then I went to the High School of Industrial
Arts, which used to be near the Waldorf-Astoria. It was way
ahead of its time. I studied music and painting, and they'd
work it so that you didn't have to be there every day, so long
as you did your work. You could go over to the park and sketch
trees. I had a music teacher named Sonberg, and he'd bring
a Victrola into class and play Art Tatum records. Imagine that!
It was around then I decided to be a singer. Of course, I'd been
singing all my life and in the shadow of show business. I had
an uncle in Astoria who was a hoofer in vaudeville and worked
for the Shuberts. He'd tell me about Harry Lauder and James
Barton and how they were humble people who had their feet
on the ground. He'd tell me about Bill Robinson and how he
had to follow him once and it almost killed him. He'd tell me
how the acts in those days honed their shows all the way across
the country and back, so that when they finally got to the
Palace in New York they were sharp and ready. I had my first

professional job when I was thirteen, at one of those Saturday-
night get-togethers at a Democratic club in Astoria, and later
I sang at little clubs by myself when they'd let me." (Harry
Celentano, a bellman at the Algonquin, who went to school
with Bennett, remembers those days: "He used to sing 'God
Bless America' and 'The Star-Spangled Banner' in assemblies,
and when he was a little older he'd go into places out there
like the Horseshoe Bar and the Queen of Hearts — this quiet,
shy little kid — and get up and sing all by himself. Some of us
would go with him, and he'd stand there and sing 'Cottage for
Sale' like a soft Billy Eckstine. We didn't take him seriously,
and we'd shout and throw peanuts at him, but he never batted
an eye. But he was also into art then. He would play hooky
and draw these huge, beautiful murals right on the street, with
chalk. Mothers and children would stop and watch, and they
were amazed. Then we'd come along and play football over
the mural, and that was that.")

Edith asks Bennett if he'd like more chicken salad, and he
shakes his head. "My first scrape with any kind of professionalism came at the Shangri-La, in Astoria, where the trombonist
Tyree Glenn had a group. He heard me singing along with the
band and asked me to come up and do a song. I think it was
Duke's 'Solitude.' I'll never forget that kindness. I went into
the service late in the war and ended up in the infantry, doing
mopping-up operations in France and Germany. My scuffling
years began to end in nineteen forty-nine, when I auditioned
for a revue Pearl Bailey was in at the old Greenwich Village
Inn. It had people like Maurice Rocco, who used to play the
piano standing up. I became a production singer in the show,

which meant I was a combination m.c. and singer. Pearl told me, 'It'll take you five years before you can handle yourself on a stage, but at least I can get you started.' Bob Hope heard me in the show and asked me to come up and sing at the Paramount Theater with him. It was his closing night, and before I went on he told me that my stage name, Joe Bari, wasn't any good, and he asked what my real name was. I told him, and he thought a moment and said, 'We'll call you Tony Bennett,' and went out on the stage and introduced me. Then he took me on a ten-day tour with him, and everybody — Les Brown and Marilyn Maxwell were in the troupe, too — showed me how to get on and off the stage without falling down, and things like that. Maybe a year later, Mitch Miller auditioned me at Columbia. I sang 'Boulevard of Broken Dreams,' and it became a semi-hit. This gave me the strength to go out on the road and work clubs in places like Philadelphia and Boston and Cleveland and Buffalo. So I'd started this crazy adventure that has lasted twenty years. Then I had hits like 'Because of You' and 'Just in Time,' and I became international in nineteen sixty-two, when I recorded 'I Left My Heart in San Francisco.' "

Edith comes in from the kitchen and says, "The doorman called, Mr. Bennett. The car's downstairs."

THE CONCERT

The concert at Alice Tully the next evening is billed as "An Evening with Rodgers and Hart," and it is a smooth and engaging success. The hall is sold out, and the audience is hip. Bennett sings the verses of most of the songs, and by the time he gets a note or two into the chorus there is the applause of recognition. He is in a dinner jacket, and his stage manner is startlingly old-fashioned: he uses a hand mike, and he whips the cord around as though it were a lariat; he half-dances, half-falls across the stage during rhythm numbers; he salutes the audience and points at it. He is clumsy and at the same time delightful. He sings twenty-one Rodgers and Hart tunes, and many are memorable. He sings a soft, husky "Blue Moon," and then comes a marvelous, muted Ruby Braff solo. "There's a Small Hotel" is even softer, and Braff and George Barnes react with pianissimo statements. The group, indeed, is impeccable. The solos are beautiful, and the dynamics all anticipate Bennett's. During Braff's solo in "The Most Beautiful Girl in the World," Bennett sits on a stool to the musicians' right, and near the end of "I Wish I Were in Love Again" he forgets his lyrics and soars over the wreckage with some good mumbo-jumbo and a fine crescendo. "Lover" is ingenious. Bennett sings it softly, at a medium tempo (it is usually done at top speed), then briefly takes the tempo up, and goes out sotto voce. He does "I Left My Heart in San Francisco" as an encore. The ovation is long and standing.

After a small backstage party, Bennett gets into his limousine and is driven home. He settles deep into a corner of the car. "It's what I used to dream of — a concert in a big hall like Alice Tully. But it hasn't all been smoothness since I started doing business. When I had my first record hits, in the early fifties, I suddenly found myself with an entourage, most of them takers. And I didn't like it. Maurice Chevalier was doing a one-man show here around then, and all he had was a piano and a hat, and that made me realize I was off on the wrong foot. Then I've been through a divorce and done a little time on the psychiatrist's couch. But I don't think I need that. Most of the people who go to psychiatrists, their hearts and minds have never caught on to any one desire. I never had that problem. But I had a different one when Frank Sinatra came out in *Life* and said I was the greatest singer around. Sophie Tucker once told me, 'Make sure that helium doesn't hit your brain,' but it did, and for several years, to match up to his praise, I overblew, I oversang. But I've found my groove now. I'm solidifying everything, and working toward my own company. You learn how to hang on to money after a while. I like to live well, but I'm not interested in yachts and fancy cars. There are things I'm searching for, but they won't take a day. I'd like to attain a good, keen intellect. Alec Wilder set one of William Blake's poems to music for me, and I was reading Blake last night. Imagine being that talented and feeling so much at the same time! I'd like to make more movies. I played a press agent in *The Oscar*, and I loved the whole make-believe about it. I'd like my own regular TV show, which would be devoted to good *music*. None of that stuff with the musicians off camera and the shots full of dancers. I like the funny things in this life that could only happen to me now. Once, when I was singing Kurt Weill's 'Lost in the Stars' in the Hollywood Bowl with Basie's band and Buddy Rich on drums, a shooting star went falling through the sky right over my head, and everyone was talking about it, and the next morning the phone rang and it was Ray Charles, who I'd never met, calling from New York. He said 'Hey, Tony, how'd you do that, man?' and hung up."

6

Aesthetic vitamins

First-rate jazz trumpeters tend to be diminutive. Consider Louis Armstrong, Bix Beiderbecke, Roy Eldridge, Charlie Shavers, Bobby Hackett, Billy Butterfield, Ray Nance, Ruby Braff, and Miles Davis. The larger the lyrical soul, it would seem, the smaller its house. This is certainly true of Braff, a five-foot-four-inch featherweight who is the most intense, inventive, and eloquent trumpeter/cornetist we have. (This is not to displace Hackett, whom Braff admires enormously; Hackett's beauties are mathematical and reflective. He is a Pope, and Braff a Blake.) In addition to being wispy and highly poetical, Braff is also rather an anachronism. He came to the fore in the mid-fifties, as part of a tradition (Armstrong, Eldridge, Buck Clayton) that had been declared dead, or at least obsolescent. Young trumpet players were no longer idolizing Armstrong; instead they followed the mercurial,

multinoted ways of Dizzy Gillespie and Fats Navarro. When Braff appeared, the fluent, florid, brilliant Clifford Brown, created largely by Navarro and killed at twenty-five in an automobile accident, was the new, young, champion trumpet player. Braff, by contrast, was a throwback, a return to an un-

fashionable way of playing that was devoted to melody, lyri-
cism, and grace. But none of this matters anymore. Gillespie's
academy grew old and gave way to the avant-garde of the
sixties, while Braff, perfecting his anachronistic form and
battling the whims of fashion and economics, has become a
tradition unto himself.

One of the marvels of Braff's style is that it has never been
overwhelmed by its mandarin tendencies. Braff is, in the best
way, a rococo performer who uses a lot of notes, sagacious
flourishes, and a scarlet tone. He favors the middle and
lower registers; daring and frequent intervals; fast, short runs;
mix-'em-up rhythmic tricks (legato/on-the-beat/double time/
legato); and melody. His use of the lower register is possibly
unique. He achieves an expansive cave of sound. ("I love the
bass and the cello," he explains. "I love the low register of the
clarinet. I love Harry Carney. I have a great need for those
sounds. I change my embouchure when I move down there,
and I move into another room, another world.") Braff is, as
well, an extraordinarily precise horn player, whose exactness
recently caused Alec Wilder to observe that "every note he
plays is the *center* of that note." Braff loves melody, and he
plays it in a rare and affecting way that lies between embellish-
ment and full-scale improvisation. He does an astonishing
thing: he does not, in the manner of many improvisers, impose
himself on the tunes he plays; rather he heats them up in such
a way that their colors and curves and textures gleam and shine.
He points up their treasures, but he leaves them intact. He will
start a slow ballad by playing the notes as they are written,
but he will celebrate them by moving along just behind the

beat in a now-examine-these-beautiful-notes slow motion. Then he will descend, suddenly and softly, into his lowest register, roam there almost inaudibly, and rise swiftly to the start of the second eight bars of the tune, which he will play on the beat but which he will alter by skipping certain notes and by adding others, in the form of miniature calligraphic flourishes. He will be more adventurous on the bridge, and, raising his volume (as the years have gone by, he has taken to playing softer and softer, without setting aside his mastery of dynamics), bob up and down through several big intervals, duck downstairs again, and then start the final eight bars a beat or two late. He will restate the melody, again gently subtracting and adding notes, and go out with a final series of low tones, the last one terminated by a soft, barely wavering vibrato.

The house that shelters these graceful sounds is oddly built. Braff's torso is shaped like a whetstone, and he has substantial feet, small hands, and long arms. His head, with receding brownish hair, is round and affirmative. He has a trumpet player's mouth, wide and rather flat, and he has heavy-lidded hazel eyes. These eyes, continually at half-mast, move slowly, like lighthouse beacons, and they dominate his face and keep his somewhat clownish nose in check. He has a surprising voice: a bowling ball in motion, it is heavy, deep, and sonorous. He is a steadily cheerful man, and his frequent chuckle has a rusty, scraping sound. When he plays, he stands motionless, his legs slightly apart, his horn pointed just above the horizon. The only parts of him which move are his lips and his fingers. He keeps his eyes mostly closed, occasionally opening them halfway and rolling them back when he takes a breath and is ready to start what is invariably a salutary phrase. He radiates the stone-stillness of absolute concentration.

Braff is obsessed by two things: he loves to talk and he loves to play. So he recently spent a perfect day, talking out the afternoon in a midtown luncheonette and playing out the evening in a recording studio, where he rehearsed rigorously with the stunning group he leads with the guitarist George Barnes.

Braff at the coffee shop: "Louis Armstrong's playing was a fat, warm, glowing thing," Braff said. "It gave me butterflies. When I got to know him, I knew I was dealing with a musical genius. He was deadly serious about music, and he had a fantastic degree of concentration and energy. Think of playing improvised music for fifty-five years! But there was no end to the amount of steam that he could turn up, even at the end. He told me once that when you play there are always two bands — the one you hire, and yourself. When the hired one is good, you turn them up mentally and dig them. But when they're not, you turn them off and *you* become the band. 'If you spend your life depending on other musicians,' he'd say, 'it's too bad for you.' Louis laughed a lot at life, like when he had that all-star group in the forties, with Sid Catlett and Jack Teagarden and Earl Hines and Barney Bigard, and he told me, 'Man, that band! Pretty soon I'm going to surprise them and let all those leaders go.' He was a very joyous host. He took real pride in making you comfortable, even in his dressing room, with fifty people standing around. He had total recall, and he loved telling stories. He'd act out every part, and I'd always think, What a pity he'll never have the chance to do straight acting roles. There was no phase of the entertainment business he didn't understand, and I *know* he could have been a great hard-core actor. He also remembered every smell and taste and feeling he'd had. He once described how as a kid he'd seen this circus trumpeter with his uniform and shining buttons and shining trumpet, and how good it made him feel, and suddenly *you* felt the way *he* did when he saw that circus cat. He also carried every bit of music he'd ever heard in his head. He was intelligent and he was tough, in that he did what he felt he had to do in this world. Louis was no cream puff. And that sense of time he had! He even laughed in time and told his stories in time. When one of his sidemen was doing his feature onstage at a concert, he'd step into the wings and tell me a story, and the last word always came the split second before he was supposed to be back onstage to play. He could play four quarter notes a certain way, and you could stand beside him and play the same notes in the same way, but your time would not be as good as his.

"Louis knew that emotion without skill is no good, and I think I've finally reached the point where the two are working together. I never used to practice at all, but several years ago I became aware that there was something wrong with my embouchure. It was very rubbery, and I had to fake certain things, like getting quickly from upstairs to downstairs on my horn. I started going to Joe Shepley's house. He's a studio trumpeter, and studio musicians don't fail when they play. I watched him practice for hours, and got inspired and started taking lessons from another trumpeter, Bernie Privin. He got me going enough so that I can practice now from the exercise books. It's hard, heavy labor — those exercises. But I play better now than I ever have. I also studied a couple of years with Sanford Gold, the piano teacher. He showed me how to take chords apart, and he showed me I could write my own things. And Louis taught me another way of practicing. 'Make up a two-bar phrase or a four-bar phrase,' he'd say, 'and keep working at it until that two-bar phrase or four-bar phrase is a complete and perfect thing, a small jewel.' It sounds easy, but it's unbelievably difficult. All this new knowledge gives me the freedom to excel, to use to the fullest what I have.

"A performer is a person who needs immediate communication and an immediate reward. Of course, you're naked when you perform. So you must always know how good or how bad you are. The only way to do that is to carry a yardstick in your head — a yardstick made up of a great Armstrong solo or of a good solo of your own — and measure yourself constantly against it. A jazz musician doesn't have time to wait around for inspiration. You create it yourself, and the way you do it is to recall something that made you happy and inspired before, like Louis' remembering that shining circus trumpeter. That way you summon up feelings of warmth and joy. And you have to keep a backlog of music in your head; you have to constantly replenish your musical supply by listening to records or the radio. This is all part of the flow of excellence, which has to be checked every day. You have to put your aesthetic vitamins in the pot every morning and stir and pour.

"Improvisation is adoration of the melody. It's imagination coupled with a strong sense of composition. The best improvisations I've heard came out of melodic thinking. When I play 'I Got Rhythm,' I play it because I love the melody, and I keep that melody singing along somewhere in my head. Running its chords doesn't interest me. What does is trying to superimpose a new melody on the original, to build in layers, like Louis did. When I play one of his records, I'm mesmerized at first with what he put on top, with the *surface*. When I play it again, I hear the second layer, and then the third. Every time I play it, I hear something I didn't know was there before. But a great solo is also this: it surprises you each time you hear it, even though you know every note by heart.

"I feel very formal about music, and that includes the way you dress onstage and the way you talk into a microphone. I used to be a wise-ass on microphone, cracking bad jokes and such, but I know now I was trying to make it with the musicians because I was insecure. There's a star system, and it shouldn't be destroyed, like the young musicians are doing now. Fred Astaire is a star. But if he'd worked in sleazy places in disreputable clothes, his talent would have suffered, and he wouldn't have star status. Look at Ellington. I get goose bumps every time that man walks out on a stage. And Goodman — the epitome of professionalism and care and tone. It's based on the understanding that you're an entertainer, and you can't be an entertainer until you play well enough to communicate with your audience. And it has to do with the American dream: if you're good enough, you'll make it because *some*body's going to pick up on you. But if you destroy the star system, what is there to shoot for? It was never the artist's job to play ugly, to parade his ugly dreams in public."

✿

When Braff drives downtown in his Toyota sports car from Riverdale, where he lives, he parks in a municipal garage at Eighth Avenue and Fifty-third Street, which he uses as his "midtown office." At eight-thirty in the evening, he gets his car and picks up George Barnes, who lives around the corner. They arrive at nine at the loft building where they will rehearse. Hank O'Neal, who has a desk job with the CIA during the day and makes records for his own label, Chiaroscuro, at night, rents a couple of floors in the building, and they contain an apartment and three huge workrooms, one of them a recording studio. He is a tall, thin, gentle Southerner, and he greets Braff and Barnes warmly. The guitarist Wayne Wright and the bassist John Giuffrida round out the quintet, and they are already there. And so are Alec Wilder and Charles Bourgeois, an altruist who divides his time between the Newport Jazz Festival organization and shepherding performers he admires. Both are great admirers of Braff. The studio has the usual jungle of cables and microphones, but there are also a sofa and comfortable chairs. A couple of thronelike leather chairs are side by side in the center of the room, and Braff and Barnes head for them. Braff has a new cornet, and he shakes it and flexes its valves and turns it this way and that. "Every new horn needs a mouthpiece made for it, and not one from another horn," he says. He chuckles and lifts his eyebrows. "And what do you know — I ain't got one. So it's going to be a bitch getting used to this tonight." Wright and Giuffrida, stationed to the rear of Braff and Barnes, are look-alikes in mod spectacles, monkish hairdos, and work clothes. They smile whenever Braff or Barnes says anything. Bourgeois, who is not happy unless he is doing something for someone else, goes out for coffee, and is told by Wright that lesser men have disappeared in the neighborhood on such missions. Barnes gets up and walks around. He is the same height as Braff, but he is ovoid. He has a round head, a small, crinkly face, and short arms. He wears his pants high, and they carry him like a vessel. He lights a giant cigar and sits down again, picks up his guitar, and rests his right foot on a brick he carries to every job. He and Braff glance at one another, Braff leans back in his chair and closes his eyes, and suddenly they are into a fast blues. The ensemble is largely in unison, and Braff and Barnes immediately melt into one voice. Braff solos first, and it is clear that he is already at the bottom of his well of concentration. Then Barnes solos. He has spent much of his career in studios, and he has a curious singsong way of playing. His notes vibrate like Django Reinhardt's, and he has an extraordinary sense of dynamics. Some of his notes are so soft they are transparent, and some ring like a clarinet's upper register. The two men exchange four-bar breaks and wing through the closing ensemble. One second of silence, then Braff cackles and says, "You see what happens when you lay off three whole weeks. Man! Let's try something else." It is Braff's own "With Time to Love," and it has a handsome melody that sounds exactly like Braff himself. When he plays it, it is as if identical twins were talking in unison. He plays very softly, the notes squeezing themselves out of the horn, and there are several deep-register phrases that suggest wine cellars. Barnes is even softer, and the room fills with gentle, stirring sounds: Braff's near whispers, Barnes' almost invisible notes, Wright's easy, quiet chords, and Giuffrida's mild, walking melodic line. The number ends with a sighing Barnes note, and he and Braff look at each other. "Hey!" Braff says. "That's togetherness!"

Braff takes a sip of coffee, and lights a cigarette. It is three-thirty, and the coffee shop is almost empty. "I was born in nineteen twenty-seven in Roxbury, a suburb of Boston. There were four children — an older brother, who was killed in World War Two; my oldest sister, who died a few years ago; and my next oldest sister, who lives in Randolph, Mass. My parents were both thrown on boats and sent over here from Russia when they were young. It was the time of the pogroms, and Jews were being slaughtered. But imagine the guts of coming to this country and not knowing the language and going to work in a factory! My mother was somewhere in her teens, and she had a sister in Boston, where my parents met. My father was the same age when he came over, I think, but he was already a carpenter and a cabinetmaker. He had a very inventive head. He once made a window where you pressed a button and it opened into the room so that you could wash it without hanging outside and breaking your neck. And when the office-furniture outfit he was working for bought a new truck, before he'd drive it he parked it in an alley and took it entirely apart, and then put it back together so that he'd know exactly how it worked. My parents live in Brighton now, and I jump up to Boston every six months or so to see them. All their records in Russia are gone, but they estimate they're about ninety, or close to it. They still have things amazingly together, far more than most of the musicians I run into at Jim and Andy's bar. About fifteen years ago, my mother decided to learn English, so she could write to me. My father long ago picked up on English because he was out in the world, but my mother has always been at home. So she started studying the newspapers, and now she writes and I can understand her. Words come out funny. She'll say 'Good lucky' at the end of a letter, and when she really gets up against it she clips out the word she wants from the newspaper and pastes it on the page. It's a Yiddish household, and I still speak it fluently.

"I knew from the time I walked I wanted to play music. But there were many, many fights about it at home. My father's father had been a clarinetist, and most musicians, outside of the symphony, were regarded as *klezmer*, a Yiddish word for a sleazy person. I wanted a tenor saxophone, and I screamed at them for years. Saxophones looked comfortable and shiny, and they had these pearly buttons. There was a strap you put on, and there was the business of choosing the right reed and wetting it and putting it into the mouthpiece. It was a sharp ritual. When I was seven, my sisters went to the Conn instrument company and looked at saxophones, but all they probably saw were baritones and such, which would have been ridiculous with my size. So they bought a trumpet. It looked silly, this puny thing with three valves and a little mouthpiece, and I felt terrible about it. But I took lessons from an old man who had been a circus trumpeter, and then he died. So I played with the radio endlessly, and that way I learned all the tunes. I never practiced from the exercise books when my family was around, because it irritated them, particularly my father when he came home from work. So I only played melodies they knew.

To this day, I use a mute in my apartment, and I can't stand anyone hearing me practice. But maybe this secretiveness helped
me get so many quiet tones on the instrument — that and the fact
I would *still* like to sound like a saxophone. The trumpet probably saved me. I felt literally imprisoned in school. I never
listened to the teachers, and anyway three-quarters of them
were not crazy about kids at all. So I continually got poor
marks, and of course I'm sorry now. I can write music faster
than I can read the papers. Recently, I've been picking up on
Alec Wilder's book about American songs, but I have to stop
every minute or two because of the big words he uses. When
I finish a chapter, I make out an alphabetical list of the tough
words and look them up and write down their meanings. Then
I take the list and go back and read the chapter again.

"I didn't get into listening to jazz until I was fourteen or
fifteen. I knew the Dorseys and Artie Shaw and Ziggy Elman
and Glenn Miller, but I didn't know Louis Armstrong or Bix
Beiderbecke. I started listening to the poolhall hustlers down
the street. They'd go to the Ray-Mor Ballroom all the time, and
they were far better critics than the real ones. They'd say:
'Oh, man, I went to see Goodman last night, and you know he
had Harry James playing lead on "King Porter Stomp," and
that's not right. And that tempo he chose for "Stompin' at the
Savoy" was way off.' They were participating, they were deep
into it, they knew everything. I began going in people's houses
who had collections of Basie and Billie Holiday and Ellington
and Armstrong. One was Mayo Duca. He was a marvelous
trumpet player and a fanatical Armstrong collector. I think
he had every record Louis ever made. In fact, Louis would

stay with him when he was working in Boston, and sit at a type-writer and write his letters and listen to his records. When you went to Mayo's house, he had a coffeepot in every room, and he'd run from room to room, drinking coffee and explaining every note on every record before he put it on, so it took all night to hear about three records.

"Around this time, I took some more lessons from a cat named Bob Gordon who came to the house every Saturday afternoon. He was a club-date trumpeter. The things he gave me I learned by ear when he thought I was reading them. I also started playing professionally at places like the Silver Dollar Bar — sometimes in the afternoon, sometimes in the evening, when I had the cab fare to get home. My parents weren't too happy about it; in fact, it wasn't until I was twenty-two that they finally gave in on my becoming a musician. In Boston, there were no steady gigs, unless you played badly. So I'd work here and there a couple of weeks at a time, and the first big-time date I had was at the Savoy, with Edmond Hall. Vic Dickenson was in the band, and Ken Kersey and that beautiful, smiling cat Jimmy Crawford. This was the late forties. I'd already been down to New York and back a couple of times, but I wasn't ready yet, and those were lean times. On one New York trip, I stayed at the Saint James Hotel, in midtown, and tried to get a day job, things were so bad. An agency sent me to a place where they made transformers. They put me in an apron, and I was supposed to wind wire around sharp, nickel-plated things, and right away I cut my fingers to ribbons. By ten-twenty, I'd had it. The next day, the agency sent me to a sweatshop where they drilled holes in pieces of wood to put Christmas trees in, and I lasted until ten-twenty-five. 'You just weren't cut out for work,' the agency said. The only gig I had during this time was a one-nighter in Allentown, Pennsylvania, with Somebody and His Smiling Irishmen. We stood all the way on the bus, and when we got there the leader told us, 'Everybody in this orchestra smiles when I smile, and frowns when I frown, and that goes whether you have a horn in your mouth or not.' Man, I thought, what have you gotten yourself into? The gig was in a ballroom, and during the first intermission I conned my pay of fifteen bucks from the guy on some pretext and ran outside and asked a cabbie what he'd charge to take me to New York. Fifteen dollars. I was back at the Saint James in two hours.

"After the Savoy date in Boston, I worked with Sid Catlett at George Wein's first Storyville there, and it was Sid who brought me to New York for good. He was something – that great big man with those little balls of drums arranged so tightly around him. He'd say, 'I can swing seventeen men with one wire brush and a phone book,' and he was right. He always had a room with a family, and he'd ask me to come to these rent parties where he lived. Two or three bucks and all the whiskey and sandwiches you could handle. I finally found out that the parties were for *him*. He loved to gamble, and he always needed bread. Before we came to New York, he took me by his place one night, and he showed me how to pack. He had two suitcases and all these camel's hair coats and twenty pairs of shoes and all, and he rolled everything into tight, perfect sausages. When we got to New York, he opened the suitcases and took everything out, and not a wrinkle! Fantastic! I've tried many times to pack that way, but my clothes come out like an unmade bed. Sid took me around town, introducing me to people, and when he played down at Bob Malz's Central Plaza, he made Malz hire me. Then, in nineteen fifty-three, I got a break. I was invited to play at an arts festival at Brandeis University, and John Hammond heard me the first time. After I'd played 'Sleepy Time Down South,' he grabbed the mike and said, 'That's *marvelous!*' John and his way of talking all the time with words like 'marvelous' and 'wonderful' and 'great.' I've had telephone conversations with him that go like this:

'Hello, Ruby. This is John. How are you?'

'Well, I'm in bed with pneumonia and I feel awful.'

'Wonderful, Ruby. Now what I called about . . .'

"Just after Brandeis, John started making his Vanguard recordings with Buck Clayton and Edmond Hall and Mel Powell, and he used me. Those records got a lot of notice, and for the first time I was on the map. I also recorded with Ellis Larkins, just the two of us, and John took it to Richard Rodgers, who was putting together *Pipe Dreams* for Broadway, and I was hired. It wasn't a speaking part. I was supposed to be an idiot wetback, but I did play a couple of times during the show. *Pipe Dreams* was based on John Steinbeck's *Sweet Thursday*, and he was at most of the rehearsals. He even got to be my coffee runner. He also told me all these wild stories. Or lies, which I guess is a writer's right. It's hard to believe that I talked with Richard Rodgers every day and watched him work. If they needed sixteen bars, he'd sit at the piano and write out those sixteen bars just like that, note for note. Then Oscar Hammerstein would fit the words to the music right away. How pleasurable it must have been for those two to work together! After *Pipe Dreams,* which lasted seven months, I worked and recorded with Benny Goodman. People say Benny is a strange cat, and I guess he is, but I got along with him. We were rehearsing at Nola Studios, and they had unhinged a big door to move an organ or something, and the door fell over on me and cut my lip so badly the doctor Benny sent me to said I'd never play again. I lost all feeling in my lips for six months, but Benny *made* me play with him every weekend at Basin Street in that little band he had with Urbie Green and Paul Quinichette. It was terrible, but it probably rescued by career."

At the recording studio, the quartet moves into a medium-tempo version of "Looking at You," and it is notable for the four-bar exchanges at the end, when Barnes mimics Braff's passages so well he makes Braff laugh. Alec Wilder, hunched forward with his chin in his hands and his eyes closed, listens intently as the four men play. He smiles at every felicitous phrase, and rears back during the fours and roars and slaps his knee. A fast "Liza" follows, and then a lullaby reading of the Beatles' "Here, There, and Everywhere." When it is over, Braff gets a glass of water, and everybody stretches. He returns and worries his new horn again. "This horn is much lighter than my old one," he says. "But I've got to get used to it. My old one, I might as well have been playing a baritone, it was so heavy. You have to be young and stupid to play one like that." The group settles down and plays a yearning version of Louis Armstrong's "No One Else but You," and I suddenly remember an equally eloquent rendition that Braff and Pee Wee Russell played one night at Newport.

In the next number, there are several starts and stops. Wright is having trouble with a tricky two-bar fill phrase. He tries it three times, to no avail, but Braff chuckles and says, "Don't worry, Wayne. There are at least a dozen out-of-work guitarists up at Jim and Andy's this very minute." Wright maneuvers the phrase, they finish the number, and everyone takes a break. Wilder and Barnes confer, and Wilder declares he is going to write a suite for the group. Barnes is delighted. Braff sits down at the piano and plays a pretty tune. "Duke heard me play this once," he says. " 'Hey, Ruby. You're going to lay that fine little tune on me, aren't you?' Isn't that something? Duke Ellington wanting a song *I* wrote!"

The coffee shop is filling up with the early-dinner, Salisbury-steak crowd. Braff orders his third cup of coffee. "The group was one of those great accidents," he says. "A couple of years back, when Bucky Pizzarrelli and George Barnes had their duo at the Upstairs at the Downstairs, I sat in with them. George knocked me out. He had a way of phrasing with me almost as if we had the same timbre, as if we were the same instrument. I kept thinking about this phenomenon, and one morning not long ago I was driving home and I stopped at Jim and Andy's on the chance George would be there. It was three-thirty, but I knew he was an insomniac. By God, he was, and we talked for a while and I said, 'Let's consolidate forces,' and he said, 'Right!' At eleven the same morning we met at his house and played for hours and had a ball. We wanted a kind of Freddie Green-Walter Page guitar and bass combination behind us, and we got Wayne Wright and John Giuffrida, and we started rehearsing like crazy. We made our first public appearance at the Newport Festival, and every notice was good. We recorded what we'd played right after, and since then we've made a record with Tony Bennett, and we're also going to do a documentary film with him, and then go into the Rainbow Grill. I've spent all my life knocking on doors, but now they're knocking on ours. So it's the right combination of souls.

"I've lived up in Riverdale for eighteen or nineteen years. I lived in Pee Wee Russell's building down on King Street before. You'd think my joint was an insane asylum to see it. I never thought it would be permanent, so I've never really furnished it. I thought I'd wait until I had an apartment in New York and one in London and one in Paris and maids and chauffeurs and then buy some decent furniture. I cook everything in a frying pan, and I cook and eat and wash up in twenty minutes. I don't think food should be too important. When I was on tour in Europe with George Wein, we'd go to a fancy restaurant in Paris and spend about three hours, and then George would say he knew another place that had fantastic desserts, and we'd go there for another hour, and then somewhere else for coffee. It sent me up the wall. I've come close to getting married a couple of times, but I married music a long time ago, and a wife would have to understand that. Anyway, there's only room for one nut in a household, and I have first claim on that.

"I don't feel right if I'm not playing, but there have been times when I haven't had a gig in six months. What I'd do, if I couldn't call a session, was go through an entire concert in my mind — an invented concert, note for note, right down to the lights and the applause. If it went well, I'd sometimes make actual notes about it: that's something to remember, something to use. But how to keep your spirits up when you're not working is another kind of discipline. One thing, I stay away from the negatives; they can bring you down and tear you apart. Another is a one-night gig. It can wipe out months of difficulty. Otherwise, it's just get through the week and then everything will be cool. But you can't abuse your music at such times by going and making a rock-and-roll record or something. If you do, your music will somewhere along the line get up and punch you in the nose. But I'm an optimist. I've always felt that things would be all right, that I'd be re-warded. I know I'm good and I know I'm unique in what I do. If I had to go out and hire someone just like me, it would be impossible, because he doesn't exist."

7

Their own gravity

During the past twenty-seven years, two smart, unassuming, strangely gifted New Englanders, born Robert Brackett Elliott and Raymond Walter Goulding, but long known in every swinging American household as Bob and Ray, have — as an amazing and unflagging repertory team — invented, fleshed out, and shepherded through the uncertain realms of radio, television, and the theater a unique company of comic characters

who bear names like T. Wilson Messy, Wally Ballou, Calvin
L. Hoogevin, Wolfman, the Worst Person in the World, Webley
Webster, Artie Schermerhorn, Chester Hasbrouck Frisbie, and
Mary McGoon, and who are in large part gentle but hilarious
takeoffs of every kind of phony, dimwit, wise-apple, bully, bore,
bungler, crook, and creep. Like many inspired inventions, the
creation of this magic company was accidental. The time was
1946 and the place the Boston radio station WHDH, where
the two men, who had never met and had just returned from
the war, were staff announcers. Bob had a morning record show
and Ray gave the hourly news reports. In the manner of Sissle
and Blake, Gilbert and Sullivan, Laurel and Hardy, and Ellington and Strayhorn, they discovered almost immediately that
they had a telepathic bond they still don't fully understand.
They speak of the same "wavelength" and the same "chemistry."
They mention such coincidences as having the same birth
month (a year apart), losing one or both of their parents when
they were eighteen, and being raised near Boston. But after
that, they look out the window and lapse into puzzled silence.
This lightning mutual understanding soon led to on-the-air
badinage, generally following the newscasts, and then to the
invention of their first comic figures: Wally Ballou, a bumbling
reporter whose voice was based on the sound of an adenoidal
New England janitor at the station; Mary McGoon, who gave
recipes and menus in a dreamy falsetto and was patterned on
Mary Margaret McBride; and Charles the Poet, the prototype
of every bad high-school English teacher, who read senti-
mental verse to organ accompaniment, and, after a stanza or
two, burst into uncontrollable laughter. Both men had long

been addicted to radio (just as the young are now addicted to the movies), and their idols included such early radio figures as Stoopnagle and Budd; Billy Jones and Ernie Hare, the Happiness Boys; Fred Allen; "Vic and Sade"; and Raymond Knight, who populated two programs, "The KUKU Hour" and "Wheatenaville," with funny imaginary figures. They also admired Laurel and Hardy, whom they somewhat resemble physically, and it is not an exaggeration to say that their roots, whether or not they are conscious of it, even go back to the hyperbolic madness of Dickens, whence so much twentieth-century humor comes. They parodied inarticulate sportscasters, pompous newscasters, rambling culinary experts, soap operas, dramatic shows (their "Mr. Trace, Keener Than Most Persons" was a takeoff of "Mr. Keen, Tracer of Lost Persons"), and such oddities as "The Answer Man." The ingenuity and variety of old-time radio has long since been replaced by three monolithic formats — news, music, and talk — so the source of much of their original material has vanished. (They are hard at work these days, though, on those radio shows built around know-it-all m.c.s who argue with and even insult telephone callers and, most recently, on television talk shows.) But a miraculous thing has happened to their comic company; instead of falling by the wayside, since parody generally exists only as long as its original does, it has taken on a life of its own and exists completely within itself, its occasional topical forays notwithstanding. Its once parasitic humor has become organic and self-renewing. The countless young people who have discovered Bob and Ray since their return to radio (WOR) after an eight-year absence, have never heard the old soap opera "Mary

Noble, Backstage Wife," upon which their daily adventure "Mary Backstayge, Noble Wife" was at first based. That isn't necessary. "Mary Backstayge" has its own laws (or non-laws), energy, motivations, and atmosphere; it is an independent comic-surrealist world. And much the same is true of the rest of their world, for it is now clear that their original parody went much further than radio: it was aimed — and still is — at plain human foolishness.

Radio is a curious medium. It is like trying to watch a play through an opaque scrim or a movie when the projector lamp fails. It renders our eyes useless while it agitates the mind's eye. In its way, it is an electronic form of the great Victorian pastime of reading aloud. Bob and Ray, forbidden the props of visual humor on radio, have made an art of comic aural effects. To be sure, they have been visible off and on, during their career on television, in the theater, and in a single movie, and they are good visual comedians. But radio is their habitat. Freed from concern over what to do with their arms and legs and faces, they can develop to the fullest the marvelous non-stop music of voices at the heart of their work — a music that is continually buttressed by myriad sound effects: explosions, footsteps, Bronx cheers, closing doors, sounds of fighting, laughter, applause, sounds of eating, and so on, many of which they once did live themselves but all of which are now on cassettes, played at the right moment by the studio engineer. Ray, who has a deep baritone, handles both the low and the falsetto voices. The gradations in each register are subtle and infinite. He uses deep, guttural tones that often explode into terrifying roars (for Captain Wolf Larsen, a remarkable creation made up of elements of the hero of Jack London's *The Sea-Wolf,* Long John Silver, and Dr. Jekyll and Mr. Hyde), a leaden voice (for bores), a light, husky voice (for lunatic pedants), a brisk, matter-of-fact baritone, close to his own voice (for manipulators), a heavy, toothless voice, which he achieves by tucking in his upper and lower lips and gumming it (for Calvin Hoogevin, a character in "Mary Backstayge," and for Webley Webster, whose main function is hanging around the studio and occasionally playing "Jalousie" on the "huge WOR pipe organ"), a flaying, grating baritone (for Commissioner Carstairs, who was introduced into "Mary Backstayge" during the Army-McCarthy hearings, in 1954, and sounded like a dead ringer for McCarthy), and, at the opposite end of his vocal spectrum, a number of falsettos, varied by subtle rhythmic displacements (for all the Bob-and-Ray females). Bob has a pleasant light baritone. He, too, is a good mimic, and has at hand Peter Lorre and various French, English, and German accents. He also has an adenoidal, pinched-nose voice (for Wally Ballou and Pop Beloved, another figure in "Mary Backstayge"), a light, floating drunk's voice (for Kent Lyle Birdley, an old-time radio announcer who gives genteel household hints — "Don't take hot food out of your mouth with your fork; sip some water instead to cool the mouth" — and drinks his way through two-and-a-half-hour lunches), and a flat, dull voice (mainly for Harry Backstayge, Mary's slow-witted husband). But there is more to their humor than these ingenious flutings. Along with parody and their special, rackety brand of surrealism, they use slapstick, sheer nonsense (the McBeebee twins, who talk in fugue form), topical humor (Wally Ballou has been running for mayor of New York, and his campaign headquarters, in a room on the ground floor of the WOR building, were closed not long ago for a couple of days while they were debugged), arcane references to old-time radio (Dismal Seepage, Ohio, mentioned not long ago on "Mary Backstayge," was borrowed from "Vic and Sade"), hyperbole, non sequitur, and surprise. They have faultless timing, and they are effortless. Dick Cavett has said, "They're immaculate performers. They're like the finest actors: there's simply too much to absorb completely in any one sequence. They have none of that sketch-playing broadness a lot of comedians fall into, and they never, never let on that they're trying to be funny. They are certainly as great as Nichols and May." Alec Wilder has studied them even more closely. "In a curious way," he says, "they are sociologists who are on the edge of being critics. By means of hyperbole, they manage the effect of defining levels of society, of cant, of pretension. They are — if there is such a word — catharsisists. They produce their own gravity, as in Newton, and they turn it off and on as they choose."

Though they are so close in spirit, philosophy, and wit, Bob and Ray are almost totally dissimilar in appearance and manner. Bob is trim and of medium stature. He has a small mouth, aquiline features, and receding, sandy reddish hair. He dresses with verve and precision. He is introverted and speculative and quiet-voiced, and his shy, slightly pop-eyed look suggests an honorably retired Scottish colonel who has recurrent nightmares about being drummed out of the regiment. Ray is as impervious as a mountain. He stands six foot two and has ample girth. Double chins, a generous nose, and smoking gray eyebrows dominate his face. His voice booms and caroms. He has an easy sense of dress, and will sally forth in a pair of light blue pin striped trousers, a purple shirt, and a gray seersucker jacket. He laughs a lot, and he walks with rapid, earth-gobbling strides. Extrovert winds seem to encircle him, giving him an openness that continually leads strangers to seek him out. Old ladies ask him floorwalker questions in department stores, and in bars he is taken for an Irish cop. The differences between the two men can be epitomized thus: When their Broadway show, "Bob and Ray: The Two and Only," opened, in 1970, they received only one bad review — a wet-fingered tirade from John Simon. Bob framed it in silver and hung it at home, which is in the East Sixties; Ray has never read it. But the two men share one physical characteristic. Like most old-line broadcasters, they are indefatigable throat clearers, and when they are in the same room the ceaseless coughs, harrumphs, and roars are almost deafening.

Few humorists are given to exhaustive autobiography, and Bob and Ray are no exception. When they talk to interviewers in their offices, on the twenty-fifth floor of the Graybar Building, on Lexington Avenue (an anteroom; a big room crammed with tapes, cassettes, 78-r.p.m. records, LPs, and recording equipment; and two small adjoining offices divided by a high partition), they have a cautious, preoccupied air. Bob is generally the first to arrive at the offices. "I was born in Boston in March, nineteen twenty-three," he said late one morning. "But I grew up in Winchester, a suburb north of the city, near Melrose. I was an only child, and so was my mother. She came from Maine, and was quite artistic. Whatever artistic talents I have — I paint watercolors and make furniture and such — came mostly from her. She did needlework and refinished old furniture and painted tôleware trays. She had an uncle who was typical of her stock: he ran a drugstore in a town of four hundred people in Maine for sixty-five years. Before he died, he gave me the soda fountain in the store, and it's a beauty. I have it in a house I have in Casco Bay. My father was an insurance man and a native of Cambridge. He was a good father, and I had great love for him, but he died when I was eighteen. He was the opposite of me. He played piano and was musical and was very unmechanical. He couldn't pound the proverbial nail in straight. I was hooked by radio when I was very young. Whenever I came to New York with my parents, we'd go to radio shows — Ben Bernie and Rudy Vallée and Raymond Knight's 'KUKU Hour.' He played a character named Ambrose J. Weems, who ran an imaginary radio station and made comments on the week's events, and he had a sidekick called Mrs. Pennyfeather, who was played by an ex-Shakespearean actress, Adelina Thomason. He also did a show, 'Wheatenaville,' in which he was a small-town newspaper editor. He was a funny man and an early influence on me, and eventually he became a close friend. He worked for Ray and me as a writer in the early fifties, when we first came to New York, and after he died I married his widow, Lee. She had two daughters, whom I adopted and who are married now, and we have three children, all still at home.

"After high school, I went to the Feagin dramatic school, in New York. It's gone now, but I think it was considered better than the American Academy of Dramatic Arts. I went in two spurts — during a summer and then for a year. Jeff Chandler and John Lund and Angela Lansbury were in my class. I worked nights as an usher at Radio City Music Hall, and later as a page at NBC, along with Gordon MacRae. Then I went back to Boston, and on the spur of the moment, in the summer of nineteen forty-one, got a job as an announcer at HDH." (Radio people have the offhandedness of all communications pros, and they like to drop the first letter of a station's call letters.) "I did everything, including remotes from places in Boston like the Silver Dollar Grill and the Seven Seas Café, where they had the big black bands. Then my father died, and I was deferred from the draft until nineteen forty-three. I was in basic training with an armored company, but when I was sent overseas with the twenty-sixth Infantry Division I was transferred to Special Services. Almost the entire armored company was wiped out. I went back to HDH in nineteen forty-six, and Ray was hired just after. I did a morning record show and he did the news, so we ran the station from six until nine. We found out almost instantly that we were on the same wavelength, and after the news we'd bat back and forth a little. The station got the rights to broadcast the Braves and Red Sox games, and they asked us to do a twenty-five-minute show before each game. It was called 'Matinée with Bob and Ray.' They had to have that rhyme, and it's the only reason we're Bob and Ray and not Ray and Bob. We started inventing our characters, and I think our first soap-opera takeoff was 'Linda Lovely.' We also got in the habit of not using a script and of ad-libbing everything. In nineteen fifty-one we had a chance, through Ray's older brother Phil,

who was with WMGM, in New York, to sub for him and Morey
Amsterdam on their weekly show, 'Gloom Dodgers.' Our stint
was recorded and became a sort of audition, and when John
Moses, who was with the booking outfit GAC, heard it, he
took it to NBC, where he had connections, and we were hired
for a daily fifteen-minute show, which ran from quarter to six
to six in the evening. We gave HDH a week's notice and took
off. They didn't *really* believe we were leaving, and told everyone that sure enough we'd be back come fall. But things were
really humming here by then. In addition to our little evening
show, we had a two-and-a-half-hour morning show and a half-
hour evening show, and in November we started an evening
fifteen-minute television show. By then, we needed some
writing help and Ray Knight had been assigned to us. It was
just about the only time we haven't done all our own stuff. The
big-gun critic then was John Crosby, on the *Trib*, and if he gave
you a good write-up you were in. He did and we were. The
chronology of what we've done since is a little foggy in my
head, but I think it goes something like this: In nineteen fifty-
three, we went over to ABC, where we had a fifteen-minute evening TV show, and the year after that we started our six-to-ten
morning radio show at INS. Peter Roberts, who's at OR now,
was at INS — in fact, he'd come over from NBC with us — and it
was there that we recorded that fantastic laugh of his, the one
we still use behind a silly record. We were at INS until fifty-six.
By that time, we had started doing live spots on the weekend
show 'Monitor,' and those lasted off and on for eight or nine
years. We also had an afternoon radio show at Mutual, on OR,
and on top of that we started the Bert and Harry beer com-

mercials for Piel's on TV. They were the stroke of Ed Graham, who was at Young and Rubicam. He came with us, and we set up the little company we have and called it Goulding-Elliott-Graham. Ed's not with us now, so the Graham has been replaced by Graybar. Around this time, we also put together an animated-film outfit, which did takeoffs of classic books and bad movies and the like, but the whole thing got so cumbersome and the payroll so long that we got out of it. We were ahead of our time is all, because it wasn't long afterward that 'The Flintstones' hit it big on TV. The Piel's commercials lasted until sixty-three, and the year before that we went on HN for an evening show, which ended in sixty-five. In sixty-six and sixty-seven, we were on the 'Today' show once a week, and then we began appearing on the 'Tonight' show. All the while, we did slews of commercials. Joseph Levine — Joseph I., not Joseph E. — had been after us for six or seven years to do a Broadway show, and finally, in nineteen seventy, we did. Frankly, when he first approached us, we were afraid, but by nineteen seventy we had more age, more bravery. It took six months to put the show together, and it was a great experience. The best review we got was in a Yiddish paper, so neither of us has ever read it, and the only bad one was that one by John Simon, in *New York* magazine. The show ran on Broadway six months, and then we took it on the road, playing places like Toronto, Philadelphia, Ford's Theatre, in Washington, D.C., Princeton, Stanford, and Fort Lauderdale. Lauderdale was unbelievable. The matinée audiences were all bluehaired ladies, and they didn't have the faintest idea what we were doing. They'd sit on their hands a while and then get up and leave.

They'd leave by the side exits, and one of them would hold the door while two or three others worked their way out, and meantime the theater would be flooded with sunlight, just about destroying everything we were trying to do onstage.

"Ray and I have never had any big differences, any major disagreements. We only see each other occasionally socially, but our families are on good terms. We all went to Hawaii once, and another time we went to Gloucester, Mass. Our teaming up has been a profitable thing. We've always been able to exist. I don't know what the hell I'd do for a living if the partnership broke up. Maybe move to Maine and be a full-time painter. One thing, I'd never go back to radio announcing, even if I could get a job."

Ray arrived, just off the short train ride from Plandome Manor, on Long Island, where he has lived since he came to New York. (The two men have always lived at least twenty miles apart, Bob preferring the city and Ray the country. And they have another habit: When they work, Bob invariably sits on Ray's right. He does on the WOR show, he did on the old WINS show, and he does in their offices. When asked about this, all Ray said was "If that's true, it must be Bob's hangup. I'd sit on his right anytime.") Sleep was still visibly rolling off him. He sat down at his desk and opened a small milk carton and drank from it. Bob went into the recording room and put a couple of 78-r.p.m.s on a tape for the broadcast that day. One was a vocal by James Barton, who gets progressively drunker-sounding on the record and becomes all but unintelligible. It is called "Floating Down the Old Green River," and Bob said they would introduce it on the show and say that it was being sung by a friend of Kent Lyle Birdley. Ray put his feet on his desk and thunderously cleared his throat. Bob echoed him in the next room.

Ray talked about his beginnings. "Well," he boomed, "I was born in March of nineteen twenty-two, in Lowell, Mass. My father was the overseer of dyeing and finishing in a textile mill. He was a pleasant sort of man, and my idol. He was always up on everything. He had the first self-starter in the neighborhood and the first radio. He'd put it out on the porch so the neighbors could listen to it. My mother was a great mimic and a great cook. There were no lumps in *her* mashed potatoes. One of my older brothers, Phil, died when he was just thirty-nine, and another one lives in Franklin Square, Long Island. My oldest sister died a year ago, and I have a younger sister in Flushing. Phil got me my first job in radio — on LLH, in Lowell. I was seventeen, and probably the youngest announcer in radio. In those days you did everything yourself. You rewrote the front page of the *Globe* for your news and the sports page for your sports. You were your own editor, you made your own transcriptions, you carried your own equipment to remotes, like the Lowell High School football games, and in particular the Lowell-Lawrence game, on Thanksgiving Day. High-school football was very big in Massachusetts then. When I was eighteen going on nineteen, my parents died, within five months of one another, and I moved in with my oldest sister. I got a job at EEI, in Boston, and a year later went into the service. I went to O.C.S., in Texas, and spent the rest of the war in Fort Knox. I hated the Army, and to make it livable I'd drive over to Louisville on weekends and work at a radio station there. I was married in nineteen forty-five, to a Springfield, Ohio, girl — Mary Elizabeth Leader. We have six kids — three grown up and three at home. I went to HDH after the war. I did the news during Bob's record show, and I began staying in the studio and bailing him out with some chatter, what with all the awful records he had to play.

"Most of our characters come straight out of our lives. Take Kent Lyle Birdley, the old-time announcer. Lately he's taken to drink. He has long, late lunches and spends most of his time across the street from the studio at a place we call the Times Square Tap. We gave him three names, so he'd have some stature. We got the idea from a list of names we saw once on a plaque — names like Ralph Moody Lancaster. Another three-namer we have is Dean Archer Armstead. He's the farm editor you used to hear early in the morning on New England radio, quoting hog prices and talking about crops and weather. Dean Archer broadcasts from the Lackawanna Field Station. Still another three-namer is Chester Hasbrouck Frisbie. He writes 'Mary Backstayge,' and he has this deep, slow, measured way of talking. He discusses coming episodes of 'Mary Backstayge' with us as if he were talking about Proust or Joyce."

Ray cleared his throat, swung his feet to the floor, and went into the recording room. Bob and Ray were asked if they were going to put the Worst Person in the World back in "Mary Backstayge." (The W. P. in the W. never speaks; instead, he makes continuous soup-slurping and crunching sounds. He is, from all implications, an ogreish and threatening figure.) Their answer afforded an invaluable glimpse into their unique improvisational techniques:

RAY: Hey, yeah.

BOB: But make him John Simon, and we'll put him on the bus.

RAY: Returning to New York from reviewing "Westchester Furioso" in Seattle.

BOB: And use the soup-slurping and crunching sounds.

RAY: That's right. Sitting there on the bus and making all these disgusting sounds next to Calvin Hoogevin.

BOB: Let me see if I can dig out the cassette with all those sounds.

The results of this exchange occurred a few days later in "Mary Backstayge," which Bob and Ray do live and off the top of their heads every day at four-twenty; it is replayed on tape at five-twenty and six-twenty. But first some background on the extraordinary tortoise paced odyssey of the Backstayges that preceded Simon's appearance.

The principal characters in "Mary Backstayge" are Mary and Harry Backstayge, a muddled Lunt and Fontanne acting team in an ageless middle age; Calvin L. Hoogevin, their next-door neighbor in Skunkhaven, Long Island, where they live; Pop Beloved, a retired stage doorman; Gregg Marlowe, who is invariably identified as "young playwright, secretly in love with Mary"; Fielding Backstayge, invariably identified as Harry's "long-lost black-sheep brother"; and his Cockney sidekick, Eddie. Harry, Mary, Gregg, Calvin, and Pop take off by train to Seattle, for the opening atop the Space Needle of Gregg's new play, "Westchester Furioso," in which Harry and Mary are starring. Disorder, which is a guiding force in "Mary Backstayge," sets in at once. Mary and Gregg have adjoining compartments on the Broadway Limited, while Harry ends up in

another Pullman and Calvin and Pop rough it in coach. A
bully provokes a fight in a nightclub in Chicago, and they all go
to jail. They are released, after pleading nolo contendere, and
entrain on the Hummingbird Special, somehow leaving Gregg
behind — an oversight that is never explained. (Loose ends
are a staple in "Mary Backstayge.") Fielding and Eddie appear
several days later, hold up the train, and steal a frequently mentioned cheap brooch Mary is wearing. (Mary's brooch is still
another arcane Bob and Ray reference to a once common radio
practice. A piece of jewelry worn by a soap opera character
would be mentioned over and over during the show, finally
taking on a kind of reality in listeners' minds. They would write
in to ask if a copy of the brooch, or whatever, was available, and
if the requests were heavy enough a piece of jewelry would be
run off by the sponsor and made available at a low cost. It was
a reasonably accurate way, in the days before instant polls, to
judge the size of a program's audience.) A character who
makes only strange African ululating sounds and is known as
The Train Buff is shot in the shoulder by Fielding when he
comes to Mary's aid, and Fielding is arrested. The trip resumes,
and the rest of them finally reach Seattle, only to get stuck in
the elevator in the Space Needle. Gregg reappears and rescues
them. Rehearsals begin, and during a scene in which Mary and
Harry are playing Ping-Pong Harry sprains his ankle and Pop
Beloved takes his place. He, in turn, sprains an ankle and lands
in the hospital, where he is put in a room in the maternity ward
with The Train Buff. Pop gets out of the hospital in three days,
but his bill comes to three thousand dollars. Meanwhile, the
play goes on, and Fielding and Eddie, working out of their

nearby mountain hideaway, try to blow up Mary and Harry by putting explosives — called "juice" — in a bouquet of flowers Harry hands Mary onstage. Wealthy Jacobus Pike — the "Wealthy" is used as a given name — arrives from New York and, being the play's sole backer, tells the cast that with the way things have been going they are closing and returning to New York by bus. The bus is decrepit and breaks down. They are put on another bus, and the Simon episode takes place:

(*Violin music*)

ANNOUNCER (*Word Carr, done in Bob's stately voice*): Next, "Mary Backstayge, Noble Wife," the story of America's favorite family of the footlights and of their fight for security and happiness against the concrete heart of Broadway. (*Music up and then under*) Today we join Mary, Pop, Calvin, Harry, and Gregg Marlowe on the bus that has just left Seattle, a few minutes after yesterday's episode, and we hear Mary say:

MARY (*Ray's falsetto*): Well, it seems to be going much better than that first bus we were on.

HARRY (*Bob, in a solemn voice, close to his own*): Yes, this is much smoother and much more comfortable. The engine sounds much more reliable, too.

CALVIN (*Ray, doing his toothless voice*): More scenic, too, this route, isn't it?

HARRY: Yes, I think that first driver started out the wrong way anyway. (*Loud collective laughter, coming from about twenty feet away*)

CALVIN: Ah, who's the group of people in the back of the bus? They keep passing around a paper bag and they all take a swig out of it.

HARRY: I don't know. They got on the bus just before we did.

They were here when we got on. They're having a good time, all right.

MARY (*sharp-toned*): Well, they seem to be having more fun than we are, I'll say that.

HARRY: Yes, and there across the aisle is John Simon. He's got his (*terrific crunching and chewing sounds*) in a paper bag. Look at the way he goes into a sandwich. Isn't that awful?

MARY (*shocked*): Right through the waxed paper and all.

HARRY: Must be hungry, I guess. (*Crunching continues*)

MARY: He seems like he's always hungry. I can't *bear* to watch him. I'm going to turn my back.

At two-fifteen, Bob and Ray walked to WOR, at Fortieth and Broadway. The studio, with its windowless, baffled walls and heavy doors, had the "blind" feeling of all radio studios. Ray took off his coat and loosened his shoelaces. Bob chose the sound effects they would need that day from a bookcase full of cassettes and gave them to Ronnie Harper, the engineer. During the fifteen-minute three-o'clock newscast, the two men sat side by side before their microphones at a big, U-shaped table and shuffled through a pile of typewritten pages — improvised material that had been recorded and transcribed during the years they have been together. At three-fifteen, after a stertorous round of throat clearings, they were off. Their show, which is sandwiched in between commercials, newcasts, weather reports, sportscasts, traffic reports, the time, and such, all of which takes up well over half the total air time, went like this:

Wally Ballou (Bob, adenoidal) appeared, and he and Ray (his own voice) discussed the debugging of his campaign headquarters downstairs. A funny vocal recording, "The Gourmet Serenade," followed. Bob (his own voice) interviewed someone who purported to be a member of their studio audience (Ray, in his light, smart-aleck voice) and who claimed that he was a troll and lived under the George Washington Bridge, and that he tried to prevent juvenile delinquents from fighting by scaring them. Mary McGoon appeared with some popovers she had just made. Ray went into a commercial, and Mary McGoon vanished. "The Gathering Dusk," another Bob and Ray serial, came next. It is done every now and then, and each episode is complete within itself:

(*Gloomy organ music*)

ANNOUNCER (*Bob, in his straight announcer voice*): And now the Whippet Motor Car Company, observing the forty-fifth anniversary of its disappearance, brings you another episode of "The Gathering Dusk," the heartwarming story of a girl who's found unhappiness by leaving no stone unturned in her efforts to locate it. (*Music up and under*) As we look in on the Bessinger household today, Edna is resting on the Ping-Pong table in the recreation room. It's late afternoon, and Dr. Nodel, the village eye, ear, nose, and throat specialist, is just arriving.

EDNA (*Ray's falsetto*): Oh, it's you, village-eye-ear-nose-and-throat-specialist-Nodel (*the words jammed together as if they were all one*). It was kind of you to rush right over and make a house call, even though I realize it's going to set me back a minimum of fifteen clams.

DR. NODEL (*Bob, in a mushy, falseteeth voice*): Well, when serious illness strikes, I don't think we should let the cost of the cure become a primary consideration, Miss Bessinger.

EDNA: Of course that's easy for you to say when I'm the one who's shelling out the cabbage. Every year my tax man marvels at the way my medical deductions run so far ahead of my gross income.

DR. NODEL: Well, of course it's true medical costs have gone up recently, but most of the patients have solved the problem by taking out health insurance.

EDNA: Well, I've dickered with a few companies about doing that myself, but I always feel too peaked to go have the physical checkup they require before they'll issue a policy. And of course none of them offer health insurance to cover the cost of getting in shape to go take the physical to get health insurance.

DR. NODEL: I'm not sure just exactly what it was you said there, Miss Bessinger, but in any event, if you're too weak to go apply for a policy, I can see how you might be regarded as a bad risk.

The molasseslike conversation continues, and finally Dr. Nodel gets Edna to tell him why he was summoned:

EDNA: I've just been scared out of my wits all day because I seem to have lost my hearing. In fact, I feel as if my eardrums are worn to a frazzle from trying to make out what you've been saying.

DR. NODEL: Well, frankly, Ma'am, I'm surprised you've been able to hear me at all. Heavy-duty earmuffs like the ones you have on generally deaden all sound.

EDNA: Oh, my stars and garters! I completely forgot I was wearing them, village-eye-ear-nose-and-throat-specialist-Nodel. I'll bet they've been causing this condition ever since I bundled up this morning to let the cat out. Well, you just can't imagine how relieved I feel to know that I'm no longer standing in — the gathering dusk.

Some typical Bob and Ray nonsense erupts:

(*Music up and under*)

ANNOUNCER: Can it be that Edna's newfound sense of hearing will at last become the turning point in her struggle against misfortune?

WEBLEY WEBSTER (*Ray, his lips tucked in and gumming it*): Hi, Bob and Ray. How's the — Oh, I'm sorry.

ANNOUNCER: Will her realization that the cat has been outside all day with its earmuffs off while she's been inside with hers on only lead to further heartbreak? Join us for the next exciting episode, when Edna finds herself face to face with a frostbitten kitten in "The Gathering Dusk."

WEBLEY WEBSTER: Sorry about that.

BOB (*in his own voice*): All right, Web. I just wanted to finish that off. I like to neaten things up, you know.

Webley Webster gave a brief report of what was going on at the Times Square Tap, and then the voice of Akbar Mytai came on. He is a character in another Bob and Ray soap opera, "Wayside Doctor," which has been dormant since they returned to radio, and he is done in Bob's Peter Lorre voice. He said he was out of work and was looking for Chester Hasbrouck Frisbie in the hope that Frisbie would have something for him in "Mary Backstayge." Webley Webster said that Frisbie was at the Times Square Tap and that he and Mytai would go and look for him. Vaughn Monroe's old theme song, "Racing with the Moon," followed, complete with Peter Roberts' taped laughter. Then Bob took a telephone call:

MME. SONIA (*Ray, in a brisk falsetto*): Hello?

BOB (*in his announcer's voice*): Can I have your name, please?

MME. SONIA: Yes, my name is Madame Sonia, and I live in Brooklyn, and I'm a first-time caller.

BOB: I don't care whether you're a first-time caller!

MME. SONIA: Well, I'm so excited because I've been calling every day and I just get a busy signal.

BOB: O.K. What opinion did you call to state this afternoon?

MME. SONIA: My opinion is that I should get a free plug on the air for the palmistry readings I give in the dimly lit parlor of my home at forty-seven thirty-eight East Blodgett Way.

BOB: No, I'm sorry. That's out of the question. We have a sales department that takes care of that.

MME. SONIA: Well, I only charge two bucks a throw, and I foretell the future and give advice to the lovelorn and predict stock-market trends and all like that. My readings are well worth the money, but I can't afford to advertise them on the radio the way I'd like to.

BOB: Well, you just spent forty-two seconds advertising them on the radio, and it's going to cost you, oh, maybe sixty dollars, whether you can afford it or not. I see the light flashing on our other phone. I'm going to take another call. You'll be getting a bill from us, Ma'am, and don't forget it.

Wally Ballou followed with a remote from Upper Darby, Pennsylvania, where he interviewed the head of the Freemex Watch Company (Ray, using his smart-aleck voice), which was about to put an electric wristwatch on the market. It would have an eight-foot cord and be plugged into the wall, and would prove so impractical that sales of regular Freemex watches would double. Bob and Ray talked about the redecorating of their studio and when the wine taps in the wall and the gold-leaf ceiling would be finished. Ray said what a beautiful view of Broadway they had out of their studio picture window. They talked about Henry Gladstone, an impeccable, longtime WOR newscaster who came out of WNAC, in Boston, along with Henry Morgan and Ed Herlihy, and revealed that Gladstone wears a smock when he broadcasts and keeps a finger bowl beside his microphone. Kent Lyle Birdley (Bob, in his soft drunken voice, punctuated with barely audible hiccups) talked about his two-and-a-half-hour lunch and said he had just seen Akbar Mytai deep in conversation with Chester Hasbrouck Frisbie at the Times Square Tap. Then came "Mary Backstayge." The moment it started, Bob and Ray seemed to draw closer at their table and a bell of intense concentration descended over them. They became extremely active; they lifted their shoulders and eyebrows, kicked their feet, and swayed back and forth in their chairs. Their in-place motions suggested the furious twitchings of dreaming dogs. They also looked at one another steadily as they slipped in and out of various voices, and when they were finished, the tension dissolved immediately in a barrage of throat clearings.

Then Biff Burns, a sportscaster (Bob), interviewed Red Finster, of Astoria (Ray, very chipper), about an upcoming automobile race, in which Finster, who has no driver's license, will drive a 1958 Edsel. Bob (stately-voiced) placed a phone call to Harlow W. Barnswell in King of Prussia, Pennsylvania. Barnswell (Ray, in a high baritone) turned out to be the keeper of a lighthouse thirty or forty miles inshore from the Atlantic. Webley Webster reappeared and began playing the opening bars of "Jalousie" on the WOR pipe organ. He was interrupted by a crying baby, whose mother (Ray's falsetto) said there was no stopping the child once it got going. Artie Schermerhorn (Ray, almost straight-voiced) did a remote from Port Washington with Professor Selwyn Hubble (Bob, in his light, husky voice), head of the Hubble Institute of Penmanship, which teaches aspiring young executives to write illegibly. They came down to Stan Lomax's usual fifteen-minute six-forty-five sportscast with a discussion of the Bob & Ray Coffeeshop, which is just along the hall from the studio and whose special that day was a single boiled potato with parsley for a dollar and nineteen cents. As Lomax began, Bob and Ray packed up, and they were out of the studio in a minute flat. They did not say good night to one another. Lomax finished fifteen seconds before seven o'clock, and Bob and Ray's celebrated signoff, on tape, resounded in the empty studio:

"This is Ray Goulding reminding you to write if you get work,

"And Bob Elliott reminding you to hang by your thumbs."

8

Hanging out with Blossom Dearie

E verything about Blossom Dearie is just right. Consider her singing. She is the youngest and least well-known of the consummate triumvirate of supper-club singers — Mabel Mercer and Bobby Short are the others — who rule the upper regions of American popular song. She has a tiny voice, smaller than Mildred Bailey's or Astrud Gilberto's or Wee Bonnie Baker's; without a microphone, it would not reach the second floor of a doll house. But it is a perfect voice — light, clear, pure, resilient, and, buttressed by amplification, surprisingly commanding. Her style is equally choice, and was once described by Rogers Whitaker as going from "the meticulous to the sublime." Her diction shines (she comes from a part of eastern upstate New York noted for its accent-free speech), and she has a cool, delicate, seamless way of phrasing that is occasionally embellished by a tissue paper vibrato. She is an elegant, polite, and often funny improviser, who lights the songs she sings by carefully altering certain tones and by using a subtle, intense rhythmic attack. Consider her songwriting. Few first-rate singers write music, and few first-rate songwriters sing. But in recent years she has produced over thirty tunes, and they are affecting extensions of her singing. Some, like "Hey, John," written after she appeared on a British television show with John Lennon, are cheerful and funny ("Hey, John, look at me digging you digging me"); some, like "Home," are ruminative and gentle and pastoral; some, like "I'm Shadowing You," with lyrics by Johnny Mercer, are works of magic: even though one may never have heard the tune before, one immediately experiences a kind of delighted melodic *déjà vu.* Consider her appearance and manner. She stands pole-straight, and is short and country-girl solid. Her broad face, with its small, well-spaced eyes, wide mouth, and generous, direct nose, has a figurehead strength. Her hands and feet are small and delicate. Angelic honey blond hair falls well below her shoulders. When she is listening, she gives continuous, receptive, almost audible nods. There is no waste in her laughter, which is frequent and quick — a single, merry, high, descending triplet. And she has a precise, almost prim manner of speaking; her sentences arrive boxed and beribboned. Consider her name. It sounds like a stage name or one of Dickens' hyperbolic marvels, but it is real. It is appropriately musical; her given name is soft and on the beat, and her surname is legato and floating. (Any other name — such as Tony Grey, which an overwrought agent once suggested — would be ludicrous.) It is also very old-fashioned; it calls to mind pinafores and lemon verbena and camomile tea.

And consider her magnetism. An old friend has said of her, "She is absolutely pure, and she will not compromise. She has this innocence that would take her across a battlefield unscathed. In a way, she resembles a Christian Scientist. If things go askew or don't fit in with her plans, they don't exist. She started getting under everybody's skin when she came back from Paris in the mid-fifties. I can't remember where she was working, but the place had Contact paper on the tables and out-of-work actors as waiters. It was funny when you'd take a new person to hear her. Her singing is so deceptively simple that at first there would be this 'Wha?' reaction, and then after a while a smile would spread across the person's face, and that would be it. You can be away from her for a long time and live your own life, and then she reappears and gets to you again. She's like a drug. She certainly has the English hooked. When she sings at Ronnie Scott's club, in London, they arrange all the chairs so that they face *her*, and there's not a sound. It's like church."

Blossom Dearie divides her year between a small Greenwich Village apartment; the family house, in East Durham, New York, where she was born; and London, whence she ventures into Scandinavia, Holland, Germany, and France. Part of her restiveness is due to economics, and part is due to an inborn need to keep on the move, to live light. Supper clubs have become almost vestigial in New York, and she is a demanding, even imperious performer who will not tolerate rude audiences. She once subbed for Bobby Short at the Café Carlyle, and, as is their wont, the swells who frequent the Café were often noisy and inattentive. Blossom Dearie repeatedly rebuked them by breaking off in mid-song and announcing, in her teacup way, "You have to be a little more quiet. Some of these people are my friends and have come to hear *me!*" The swells responded by staying away, and business was poor. But a while ago she surfaced again at Three, a bar and restaurant on East Seventy-second Street, and I called to ask if I could visit her in the Village. She suggested that I come in the morning, so that we could "hang out together for the day."

She lives in a one-room apartment on the third-floor front of an old building facing Sheridan Square. When I arrived, the room was knee-deep in sunshine, and she was brewing Irish tea in her Pullman kitchen. The apartment, which has a *pied-à-terre* look, is furnished with a convertible sofa, a couple of yellow director's chairs, a small round sidewalk-café table, an upright piano, a tiny white desk, a record player, and several shelves of records. Blossom Dearie put two mugs of tea on the table and sat down. She was wearing black pants, a white turtleneck, and a patterned black and off-white cardigan sweater. She laughed, crossed her legs, and rested her clasped hands on one knee. "I've decided I want to live a long time," she said. "A very long time. So I'm very conscientious about taking care of myself. I read Carlton Fredericks and Adelle Davis, and I take vitamins, especially Vitamin E, which is the wonder vitamin and helps retard the aging process. And I go to bed early and get up early. I can't stand the all-night nightclub thing anymore, and anyway what reason is there for a single person like me to stay up late? So I've invented a new kind of show at Three. In fact, it's been tried at Reno Sweeney, here in the Village, and maybe it'll catch on elsewhere. Since I don't feel I can devote all my time to performing anymore, I work just four days a week, and what I do is give an early evening concert. It starts at six and ends at eight. That way people can go out and hear me and have dinner and go home to bed. No drinks are served when I sing, but there is an intermission. I've been cracking since six this morning. I've transposed a new song into my key and nearly learned it, and I've practiced Billy Strayhorn's 'Lush Life,' which I've avoided for years because it has such poor lyrics. But it is a beautiful and quite complicated song. I've called London twice. I've written Norman Granz, asking if he can help me get the rights for the seven albums I made for him, so that I can reissue them. And I've written two of the eleven girl friends I regularly correspond with in foreign countries. I've had a business conference with Joyce Ackers, who's doing publicity for me. I've talked to Candace Leeds, at Town Hall, about my Interludes concert. I'm trying to get my life beautifully organized, and I have several projects under way. One is starting my own place, which Joyce is working on now. I don't want to buy a building or anything, just rent a room. It's going to be *scientifically* done. I want perfect acoustics, so that people *can* talk but won't bother me. You'd be surprised what a performer can hear — every word, every whisper. There will be the right kind of ceiling and perfect ventilation, so that there won't be that horrible smokiness. And the lighting will not wear my eyes out. Another project is getting my own record label going, in addition to reissuing the Granz things. Some of my wealthy friends have dropped hints about investing in it. I already have my own publishing company. I thought for a while of calling it and the record company Joie de Vivre, and a friend suggested Fragile Publishing and Fragile Records. But I've settled on Blossom Dearie Publishing and Blossom Dearie Records. And, finally, there are my songs, my composing, which has become very important to me. So important that I only want to collaborate with lyricists like Johnny Mercer. I have some new songs for him, but he's in Europe, writing a show with André Previn. He sent me a marvelous letter a little while ago, celebrating our friendship, and saying that since we'd survived folk rock and soft rock and hard rock we'd go on forever. It really pleased me."

Blossom Dearie laughed, and abruptly stood up. "I'd make another cup of tea, but I have to tape part of the sound track for an industrial film for a friend of mine, and the date starts in twenty minutes. The studio is on West Fifty-second Street." We walked to Sixth Avenue and got a cab. "I have a method now when I compose," she said on the way uptown. "I write out the rhythms first, almost like a piece of drum music. Then I put the melody to that. Songs come to me in different ways. I've written quite a few of what I call tribute songs — songs for people I admire, like John Lennon and Tony Bennett. These songs are pure inspiration, pure communication between my brain and fingers and my admiration for the person, and generally they come to me quickly. Otherwise, I jot down ideas — three bars, eight bars, maybe ten — and work them out at the piano. I keep playing them over. I play them in the morning and I play them in the evening. I play them when I've had a drink and when I haven't. But I set myself a time limit.

I'll work on a song for two weeks, and if it doesn't come out right I put it away for a year. But sometimes even that doesn't help, and the song never works. There's a lot of freedom now in writing songs. You don't have to follow the old thirty-two-bars-with-a-bridge pattern anymore. Songs can be any shape or length. They can be in sections or little movements. They can be a kind of string of ideas."

The recording date was in Studio B of Aura Recording, Inc. Two of the three accompanists Blossom Dearie had chosen — the reedman Hal McKusick and the bassist Jay Leonhart — were already there and noodling away on opposite sides of the room. McKusick, ruddy-faced and wearing round, gold-rimmed spectacles, is in his late forties, and came up through the big bands. An enormously able musician, he favors the alto saxophone, the clarinet, the flute, and the bass clarinet. Leonhart is in his twenties and is well considered. McKusick told Blossom Dearie he had moved from the city to Sag Harbor six months before and was restoring an old house he had bought. He said it had seven fireplaces and so many rooms he didn't know what to do with them. Blossom Dearie was listening and nodding, and then she said, "Marian McPartland told me she's so tired of living in small places where you have to have the piano in the same room with you all the time."

"And the bed under the piano," McKusick added.

Blossom Dearie laughed; then, suddenly, she was all business. She passed out lead sheets to McKusick and Leonhart and sat down at the piano, which was wedged in a far corner of the studio. Only her pants legs and the blond top of her head were visible. The recording involved her playing and singing two choruses of Harold Milan's "Going Away." She ran through the tune once with McKusick, who played the melody on flute behind her. When she had finished, she peered at him over the sheet-music rack on the piano and said, "Does that sound right?"

"Very close," McKusick replied.

"All right, let's do it again," she said, in a commander-in-chief tone. "And maybe you should improvise behind me, Hal, instead of just doing the melody."

"I think I'll switch to the alto flute this time," McKusick said. "I brought it along because I suspect it will fit very well with your sound."

After the runthrough, Blossom Dearie said she was delighted with the alto flute, which has a smoky, enfolding timbre. She got up to greet her third sideman, the drummer Al Harewood, who is short, compact, and a spiffy dresser. They embraced, and she laughed and told him the date would be heavy rock and roll. A tall, sandy-haired A. & R. man, Gordon Highlander, appeared, and outlined to Blossom Dearie what he wanted in the first chorus — a cheerful tempo, quiet drums, and a strong beat. As soon as Harewood was ready, they played the tune again. Blossom Dearie's unamplified voice was being drowned out by her own accompaniment, and all hands put on headphones so that they could hear her. Two takes were made, and the second was played back. It sounded marvelous. Her voice was sweet and exact, and the flute set it off like the ring around a rain moon. Two more takes were made, and Highlander said they had it.

"Take five minutes," Blossom Dearie ordered. She went up

to the window of the control booth and, a little girl standing in front of a toy shop, said, "Have you got any tea or Danish in there?" There was no answer, so she went around the corner and into the booth. McKusick and Leonhart started a fast, light version of Charlie Parker's "Confirmation," and Harewood joined in, dropping contented bombs on his bass drum. The date resumed, but this time thirteen takes were needed before Highlander was satisfied. It was two-thirty. Blossom Dearie took down her musicians' addresses and filled out the necessary tax and union forms. McKusick told her how fine she sounded, and thanked her for the chance to work with her. He and Leonhart left together, and Harewood, after packing up his drums and embracing her again, followed.

"Al is a terrific drummer," she said. "I've worked off and on with him for years, and he can play any kind of drums. And with so much taste." Highlander reappeared and told Blossom Dearie that, after all, they would need some overdubbing — just the title of the song. She looked tired but nodded. She sat on a high stool in the middle of the studio, and, putting on headphones and raising her chin, sang five "Going Away"s. Highlander asked her if she would sing with a little more rubato. She did.

We took a cab back to the Village, and on the way I asked her if she would like some lunch. "That would be nice, very nice," she answered. "I don't eat at night after work, but I do like a nice lunch. There's a new place around the corner from the Village Vanguard, called the Caffè da Alfredo. Let's try that." The Alfredo, which is on the parlor floor, looks out through big windows onto Seventh Avenue. It was crowded, and the only empty table was in the rear. "Oh," Blossom Dearie said. "I was hoping to sit right up front by a window, where there's lots of light and you can see everything. I hate sitting in the dark backs of places. I like light and sunshine and air." We sat down anyway, and then four people got up from a front table. "Let's go up there," she said. The table was loaded with glasses and dishes, and she asked the only waiter if we could move. He looked annoyed and shook his head. I thought that she would sit there anyway. But all she did was let out a long "Well" and look at the menu. She ordered pea soup and a Niçoise salad, and so did I. Alfredo's doesn't have liquor, so I went out for a half-bottle of Soave Bolla. Blossom Dearie was attacking the bread when I got back. I poured her a glass of wine, and she said it hit the spot. She broke off a piece of bread and took another sip of wine, and the soup, teeming with real peas, came.

"All I could think about up there in that studio was my mama. She passed away a little while ago. In fact, I've just come back from the country, and tonight will be the first time I've worked at Three in several weeks. I think they've told everyone that I've closed, so there probably won't be anyone there. My mother was in her late eighties, and she was a wonderful woman. She came over as a little girl from Oslo, where she was born. Her father was in the merchant marine, and she was raised by a grandmother. She married a rich man in New York, and they lived on West Twenty-second Street and had a house in the country — the same house she died in. It was a two-day trip in those days — up the Hudson by steamboat and twenty more miles by horse and buggy. After her husband died, she moved to the country for good. She met my father up there. When I think of my daddy — well, he was just one of those people who never seem to find their way, who never get into the niche meant for them in life. He was in the First World War, and then he was a bartender for the rest of his life. He was a lovely man. He was from Irish and Scottish parents. The name Dearie goes back in Scotland to the sixteenth century. People ask me over here if it's my real name, but everybody over there knows it. My daddy had the Irish wit — he could mimic anybody — and he was musically gifted. He could sing and dance, and he wanted to be in show business, but I guess he just didn't know how, and anyway he was not aggressive and was very much involved in his families. He had been married before, and both he and my mother had children in their earlier marriages. She had three boys, and he had one. I was their only child. It was he who named me. I was born in April, and the day I arrived a neighbor brought over some peach blossoms, and when my father saw them he said, 'That's it. We'll call her Blossom.' My mother liked Victor Herbert, but she wasn't musically inclined. She'd take me on her lap when I was two or three, and I'd pick out real tunes on the piano. I took my first piano lessons when I was five, from a Miss Parks, who lived three or four miles up the mountain. She taught me how to read. Later, I spent some time down in Washington with one of my brothers, and I studied there with a Mrs. Hill. For a year. She'd play Bach and Chopin, and if I liked it she'd tell me to learn the piece. Too many piano teachers force-feed their students. She wanted me to be a classical pianist, and thought I should study at the Peabody Conservatory, in Baltimore, when I got old enough. But I went back to the country, and I didn't study after that. I played with the high-school dance band, and I listened and listened — to Count Basie and Duke Ellington and Art Tatum. The first singer that made a real impression on me was Martha Tilton.

"After I graduated from high school, I came to New York. I had spent a little time here before, and I'd met Dave Lambert, the singer. It was the late forties, and I lived in a midtown hotel with a bunch of girl singers. I started to sing for the first time in New York. I hung out with Dave, and we rehearsed and talked a lot about singing. And I hung out in that basement apartment Gil Evans had on West Fifty-fifth. I don't know how he ever got anything done, because there were people there twenty-four hours a day. Charlie Parker lived there for a while, and you'd generally find Dizzy Gillespie and Miles Davis and Gerry Mulligan and John Lewis. Or George Handy would be there, or George Russell or Barry Galbraith or Lee Konitz. I'd go over to Fifty-second Street, and hear Bird and Diz. Do you remember Parker's first recording of 'Embraceable You' — the take that goes like this?" She hummed the most famous version note for note — a feat, considering that it is also one of the most subtle and difficult improvisations ever recorded. "Then I began getting jobs around New York. I was in the Show Spot, which was underneath the Byline Room, where Mabel Mercer was singing. I played piano and sang and accompanied other singers. I still like to accompany friends who sing."

The salads, which were huge, arrived, and Blossom Dearie

dug in. I poured more wine, and she buttered the last piece of bread. "In nineteen fifty-two, when I was working at the Chantilly, I met Nicole Barclay. She and her husband owned Barclay Records, and she asked me if I'd like to work in Paris. I said yes, and took the boat. I stayed with Nicole's grandmother and studied French at Berlitz. I worked in the Mars Club in Paris, and with Annie Ross at a club in London. I formed a group called the Blue Stars of Paris; the Swingle Singers eventually grew out of it. There were four boys and four girls. The boys played instruments and sang, and the girls just sang. We had Christiane Legrand, Michel's sister, and Bob Dorough, who was in Paris accompanying Sugar Ray Robinson. We had a hit record — 'Lullaby of Birdland' sung in French. There was a marvelous ambience in Paris then, an easy, hanging-out-in-cafés ambience. Bud Powell was around, and so was Don Byas. I met Norman Granz, and he recorded me there. And I met my husband, Bobby Jaspar. He was playing flute and tenor saxophone where I was working, and we became friends right away. He came from a wealthy Belgian family, and he had a degree in chemistry and spoke three languages. His father was a well-known painter. We were married in Liège, in nineteen fifty-five, and came back here the following year and lived in the Village. He worked with Miles Davis and J. J. Johnson. Then we separated. He had a heart condition and became ill, and he died. It was all very sad. I hope someday to get married again.

"For the next several years, I worked around New York, at the Village Vanguard, opposite Miles Davis, who became a great friend, and the original Upstairs at the Downstairs. Then I heard the album of *Beyond the Fringe*, with Dudley Moore and Peter Cook and Jonathan Miller and Alan Bennett, and I was crazy about it. I met Dudley Moore at the Vanguard one night when he was working there, and he asked me if I was English, and I said no, but that it was a great compliment that he had thought so. We talked until five in the morning at the Vanguard, and it was through Dudley that I eventually got back to England. The English audiences seemed to take me in and like me, and I've been going every year since. In nineteen sixty-six, I started working for a month every summer at Ronnie Scott's club. The only thing I don't like about it is that the first show isn't until *eleven-thirty* and I don't finish until two. But I just sleep a little later in the morning to make up for it."

I told Blossom Dearie it was five o'clock. "Oh, my," she said. "I'll just run home and get dressed and put on some makeup. You go out and poke around, or something, and pick me up in twenty minutes. I like to get to the club real early." She was all in blue and white and gold when I arrived. She was wearing a long royal blue gown with white cuffs and a white Peter Pan collar, and her neatly parted hair shimmered. She handed me the sheet music of "Lush Life," and, sitting down at the piano, asked me to prompt her. I prompted her twice, and when she was several bars from the end she stopped again. "I just don't like the word 'rot' there. I hate it, and I won't sing it." I suggested "die" instead. She thought a moment. "Good! I'll try that." After she finished the song she said, "I think that works. All right, off we go!"

Three is a long, narrow brick-walled place with a bar up front, a kitchen in the middle, and a small, square room in the back. The back room has an upright piano centered on one wall and facing a dozen tables. Joyce Ackers met us in the bar and said that she had spent the day trying to get the word around that Blossom Dearie would be singing that evening. She turned to me: "Anyway, Jean Bach, who produces Arlene Francis's radio show on WOR and is an old, old friend of Blossom's, is coming with a friend, and so is Harold Taylor. He used to be head of Sarah Lawrence, and he's an educational bigwig now. He's bringing Viveca Lindfors, who's dying to hear Blossom. And there may be a couple of other people." The friends arrived around six, and after Blossom Dearie had chatted with them she went into the back room and played by herself for ten minutes. Then she came out and said it was time. All nine or ten of us — several people had come in off the street — trooped into the back room. A heavy black curtain was drawn across the door, the lights went down, and she started in with "Ask Yourself Why," by Michel Legrand. She has a busy, luminous, childlike look when she sings. Her brow furrows from time to time, and she rocks continually from side to side, as if she were beating twenty egg whites. She is a superb, swinging accompanist, and her piano sometimes suggests the intense, pushing backgrounds of John Lewis. Her eyes flicker back and forth between her hands and her audience. A funny song by Bob Dorough and Dave Frishberg, "I'm Hip," was followed by the Legrand-Johnny Mercer "Once Upon a Summertime." Then she did three of her own songs — "I'm Shadowing You," "Hey, John," and "I Like You, You're Nice." Before her next number, she said to the room, "What's that noise?" There was a remote humming sound. Joyce Ackers said, "It's the kitchen fan. I'll see what I can do."

Blossom Dearie laughed, and started "The Girl from Ipanema." She ended the first part of the concert with another funny Frishberg effort, "Peel Me a Grape." The applause was prolonged and loud.

Blossom Dearie went into the bar, and Harold Taylor bought everyone a drink. She ordered a brandy, and we sat down. "Well, it took a while to get going," she said. "I'm a very gentle singer. I'm not a belter. But I try and put feeling into my songs. What I do in my way Streisand and Minnelli can't do. After I've decided how to sing a song, I sing it almost exactly the same each time, so I don't improvise while I'm singing; it's a quality I don't have. But Annie Ross has it. She can get up and sing any song in any place and knock you right out. She's so impromptu it's unbelievable. My mind wanders when I sing. I think about all sorts of things — my mama or a particular person in the audience. I think about the composer or the lyricist or one of my musicians — when I can afford to have them, that is. The words become automatic. I get nervous when I perform, but I'm told I always look perfectly calm. But then I'm a very normal person. I'm not a show-business person. I don't have the ego for that. I'm not neurotic, and I'm not crazy. I've just worked on my career. There have always been hard times financially, but perhaps all my projects will get things off the ground now. I'd sort of like to become the rage for a while."

9

The president of the derrière-garde

In the spring of 1972, Alec Wilder committed his finest ironic act: he published an invaluable and pioneering book, *American Popular Song: The Great Innovators, 1900–1950,* in which he examines, with wit and grace, some eight hundred of the three hundred thousand American songs submitted for copyright in the first half of the century, and in which the work of Alec Wilder is nowhere mentioned. But irony has long been a way of life for Wilder. He is a man of Johnsonian prin-

ciples and persuasions, who is extraordinarily timid and almost completely lacking in self-confidence. He lives a semi-nomadic existence, even though he is steadfastly responsible and loyal to his friends, and he has avoided the limelight so assiduously that he has become famous for it. He is in his late sixties and delicately constructed, but he has the vitality and curiosity and strength of a child. He detests violence, but, full of Martini courage, he once challenged a famous bandleader to take off his glasses and step outside. He has repeatedly run away from opportunities to make sizable sums of money, not because he dislikes money per se but because he refuses to blow his own horn or sully himself in the marketplace. And now he has written a book which, because it is probably definitive, threatens to send his popular songs into oblivion once and for all. (An appendix dealing with Wilder's work and written by a sympathetic critic would not have been unseemly; Wilder, though, would have roared incredulously at the notion.)

That the book was completed at all is a miracle. It was edited, with an introduction, by Jim Maher, a man of imposing patience, erudition, and intelligence. He talked a while ago of how the book came into being: "Alec had had the idea for years, but it didn't jell until nineteen sixty-seven. He applied for a grant. Silence. Then he contacted me, and since I'd had some experience with foundations, I wrote an exhaustive backup letter, full of cost estimates and couched in mahogany academese, and we got the grant. This was in nineteen sixty-eight. I suggested the structure of the book and got together the raw materials — sheet music, what shows songs had been in, what movies, whether or not a song had been dropped from a show, and so forth. We screened some seventeen thousand pieces of sheet music, and after that we interviewed those composers who would talk to us. Richard Rodgers was polite and I think not a little fascinated, and Harold Arlen was marvelous, but Irving Berlin was — let us say — intractable. Then, whenever Alec was in town, we'd retire to Howard Richmond's office, on Columbus Circle — he's Alec's publisher, and a saint — and Alec would sit down at the piano and shout, 'Come on! Come on! Let me get going!' I'd lay out all the tunes by a specific composer, and he'd play through them and make comments. I'd jot them down and ask questions in return. When he'd finished, I'd type up what he'd said and send it to him, along with the appropriate sheet music. Writing like a madman, he'd fill spiral notebook after spiral notebook, which I'd transcribe. Then we'd revise. I was terrified when he came to my apartment to go over the Jerome Kern chapter, which is the first big one. I had a query every two sentences, but he took it with pleasure and fun, and in two days and two nights we had it done. It was the initiation, and after that the sailing was smoother."

The book is a fair, positive, scholarly celebration of American songwriting which comes down hard but graciously on the insufficient and applauds the good with lyrical aplomb. Wilder writes of Jerome Kern's "The Song Is You": "It is, I'm afraid, one of Kern's self-consciously elegant 'art songs'; it attempts too dramatic a statement on too small a stage. And it suggests a grander voice than that usually associated with popular theater music. It borders on the vehicle-for-the-singer more than the song-in-itself, and, to carp one last time, it employs rubato as opposed to steady tempo." Later on, he embraces Harold Arlen: "His songs made me feel that I had a friend in court, and that were we to meet, he would be sympathetic and even encouraging. I envied his talent, but, strangely, I never tried to write in his fashion. I sensed that he lived at the heart of the matter, where the pulse was, and that I was an enthusiastic outsider. And I was right." Wilder continually demonstrates the insight that only a first-rate composer could have into the work of his peers. On Cole Porter's lyrics: "They seldom risked or indulged in tenderness or vulnerability. Even when concerned with emotional stresses, they often managed to keep at a polite distance from true sentiment by means of a gloss, a patina of social poise . . . Or else they resorted to melodramatic clichés. The light touch, the mordant turn of phrase, the fingertip kiss, the double-entendre, the awareness of the bone-deep fatigue of urban gaiety, the exquisite, and the lacy lists of cosmopolitan superlatives — these were the lyrical concerns of Cole Porter." And at last the score of *South Pacific* is put in focus: "I'm sorry to say that the melodies from *South Pacific,* immensely popular though they were, took on a kind of self-consciousness that is akin to . . . Kern's . . . I almost feel as if I should change into formal garb before I listen to them. Or it may be that I've stopped believing. Something's missing: fire, impact, purity, naturalness, need, friendliness, and, most of all, wit." And a passing but highly perceptive comment: "Of all the better songwriters, I can think of very few who have any emotional kinship with the jazz musician and his bittersweet, witty, lonely, intense world." Along the way, Wilder sets down his principles, which are lofty and ringing: "I should make clear that my criteria are limited to the singing (melodic) line and include the elements of intensity, unexpectedness, originality, sinuosity of phrase, clarity, naturalness, control, unclutteredness, sophistication, and honest sentiment. Melodrama, cleverness, contrivance, imitativeness, pretentiousness, aggressiveness, calculatedness, and shallowness may be elements which result in a hit song but never in a great song."

Wilder has steadily applied these principles to his own work, which comprises an astonishing canon. He has, with amusement, called himself "the president of the derrière-garde," but he is a unique and adventurous composer, who has written a huge body of music, both popular and formal, most of it nearly unknown. Among his works are several hundred popular songs, three of which became hits in the mid-forties and are now standards — "I'll Be Around," "It's So Peaceful in the Country," and "While We're Young." His songs have an airy, elusive quality quite unlike that of any other American songwriter. The melodic lines flicker and turn unexpectedly, moving through surprising intervals and using rhythm in a purposeful, agile, jazz-based manner. The songs have a sequestered, intense gentleness, a subtle longing for what was and what might have been that eludes most ears and that demands singers of the rank of Mabel Mercer and Frank Sinatra and Mildred Bailey and Blossom Dearie. (Wilder is obsessed with the need to have singers sing his popular songs *as written.* This does not often happen. Sometimes singers consciously change notes, perhaps thereby improving the melody, and sometimes they accidentally change or omit notes and warp the song. The trouble with this, in Wilder's view, is that other singers pick up these alterations and in turn are imitated. Yet — another Wilder irony — he is an impassioned student of jazz.) In a rare way, Wilder's melodic lines savor the lyrics at every turn, and, indeed, they are often written to fit the words, which have been done by Wilder himself and by such craftsmen as William Engvick and Johnny Mercer. In the early fifties, Wilder, after hesitating for years, plunged with vigor into the world of formal music, and the variety and scope of his compositions are be-wildering.

Trying to place him in the world of formal music is equally bewildering. Jim Maher has said of him, "One must, in Alec's case, let uniqueness be unique. He occupies his own space in the world of formal music and that's it. He writes mainly for wind instruments, and the academic community tends accordingly to look at his pieces as divertissements, as entertainments. They also regard him as frivolous because he is primarily a melodist, a composer who thinks in terms of timbres and coloristic things. You see, he had little formal training and his gods have always been Bach and Debussy and Fauré and Ravel. But if he is wholly outside the academic community, he is revered by the great performers, like John Barrows and Harvey Phillips and Bernard Garfield. He is a major figure to them, and they gossip about him the way the English gossip about the Queen." He has written for full orchestra and for wind ensembles, he has written choral works and chamber music, and he has written operas, operettas, and concert songs. (He works at enormous speed. Recently, in a matter of six months, he completed two trios for bassoon, clarinet, and piano; a suite for French horn and orchestra; a suite for flute choir; his eleventh woodwind quintet; a euphonium concerto with a woodwind ensemble; and a dozen piano pieces each for Marian McPartland and Ellis Larkins.) His love of chamber music is boundless. He has written for every instrument in the orchestra, and in extraordinary combinations. There are woodwind-and-brass quintets; trios for oboe, clarinet, and bassoon, and for clarinet, French horn, and piano; suites for string bass, tuba, and piano, for three guitars, for trombone choir and clarinet choir, for French horn, tuba, and piano, and for two oboes and two English horns; sonatas for bassoon and piano, for alto saxophone and piano, for tenor saxophone and strings, for euphonium and piano, and for tuba and piano or orchestra; and concertos for baritone saxophone, French horn, and woodwind quintet, and for tuba-and-wind ensemble. All these chamber works have been played and some have been published, but very few have been recorded. One that has is a suite for French horn, tuba, and piano. It was written, as all Wilder's formal music now is, for specific players, in this case John Barrows (horn) and Harvey Phillips (tuba). Bernie Leighton, who appears often on Wilder's records, is on piano. The piece, in five movements, is of a high lyric order. It easily converts the tuba from a two-by-four into a soaring gable; it demonstrates Wilder's singular melodic gifts and it makes it clear that Wilder has succeeded where so many have failed — in making jazz and formal music work hand in hand. (His pop melodies and formal melodies are sometimes almost interchangeable. He thinks of them this way: "It's mainly a matter of degree. The seed of a song grows into a small plant with a single flower, but a concert piece has as complex a root system as a tree.") Of particular note in the suite are the second movement, which is mournful and elegiac, and in which the two horns move in subtle, close counterpoint in such a way that it is sometimes difficult to tell one from the other, Wilder having written high for the tuba and low for the horn; the third movement, which is built around a cheerful seven-note riff, and in which the horns, swinging very hard, pursue and echo one another; and the last movement, which starts as a fugue and dissolves into long, intertwined melodic lines that are capped by a clapping, dual harrumph.

When I called Wilder at his pied-à-terre, the Algonquin Hotel, to find out whether I could visit him, he told me in a round-about way that the dental crisis of his life had arrived and that he would not be able to talk to me — if, indeed, he was ever able to talk again — for several weeks. He said the deed — the installation of false teeth — would be done in Rochester and that he would recuperate at a friend's house in Cambridge. But he is not a quiescent man, and a week later a letter from him arrived. Then came another, and another. Before he got back to New York, they were coming almost every other day, and they formed a marvelous overture that made one impatient for the principal work. The letters had a fine, eighteenth-century timbre. Some were broadsides, some were inchoate, some were confessional, some were mystical and some very funny. And they were rhetorical; no answer was expected, or even possible. After a while I began putting subject titles on the letters, some of which go this way:

ON BEING A CURMUDGEON

In spite of my need of the leavening of laughter, I am hourly infuriated by stupidity, indifference, lack of style, obeisance to faddism, obsessive competitiveness [and] middle-class concepts such as relevance, the meaningful, and the significant.

My only ambition is to be a better person and a better creator. It's increasingly difficult, but I attempt to keep an open mind and a hungry heart, a constant need for wonderment and magic. While I acknowledge the validity of honest giving, I'm also aware of the grace of receiving (not taking). I'm a fiend for order, self-discipline, and morality. I despise anarchy in living as much as art. I do not equate the new or the original with the superior. I believe in interdependence, and, therefore, tradition.

I gave up alcohol primarily to avoid the risk of false-courage anger, and have, thus far, managed to maintain a degree of benignity, except for ill-timed boiled eggs — and that new grotesque hero: the common man. Civilization, such as the dear sickly creature is, lies in the ditch starving to death and waiting not for the wise man, the creator, the forest ranger, the anthropologist, the entomologist, the philatelist, the numismatist, the dancer, the leprechaun, the bird-watcher, or Evangeline Adams but for that indulged, cosseted, adulated, protected, and idealized idiot — the common man! Who in hell started this macrocosmic love-in? Schweitzer? Burns? (Didn't he come up with "man's inhumanity to man"?) Steichen, with his "Family of Man"? What about the deserving, the *uncom*mon, the excellent, the striving, the visionary, the come-hell-or-highwaterer? Must he sigh patiently, lovingly, understandingly, waiting . . . until the new, complacent, vainglorious hero stumbles into sight? [But] I suppose the nobility who were privileged to listen to the premières of the Brandenburg concerti were a pretty vapid, unwashed lot.

A less congested letter came the following day. Wilder's diatribes, I was to learn, are like line squalls — wild, intense, loud, and over almost before they have started.

ON PRIVACY AND MONEY

As the giant spring coils tighter, people, even good friends, listen less and less. And strangely, not just because they, too, want to talk. I watch their eyes glaze; I don't believe they're spinning fantasies to themselves or plotting devious deals. It's some dreadful form of autohypnosis, turning on without drugs, their conscious mind blocked by too many garish likelihoods.

I ask myself: Is privacy (in these turbulent times) like keeping a line warped to a dock because if you release it the motor may fail, the sails jam, the oars break? Those who revel in publicity and being written about are delighted with the high seas and no charts, for they know they'll be surrounded by all their buddies in a similar situation — not, to them, a plight or a crisis, rather the great roiling arena. I'm a small-pond person: I hate danger and am horrified by violence. I've never sought more excitement than can be found in an amusement park, and that only after others' insistence.

Judy Holliday, while listening to some new quintet or sonata [of mine], would suddenly point at me and say, "That's the special passage, the secret love, isn't it?" And of course she'd always be right. Yet they weren't secrets to be hidden but secrets to be shared, secrets because they were very delicate and needed stern and unremitting protection.

Years ago I solved the problem of publicity by playing the buffoon whenever I was interviewed, and by means of hyperbole I gave the writers what they wanted: the label of eccentricity. It didn't require much effort. When you live alone most of the time, avoid groups, parties, public functions, I guess you do develop odd ways. But I never told them much, very simply because I knew they were only half-listening and would be exasperated and possibly angry if I persisted in presenting my true self. Mine is not a large landscape; I live like one of Sally Carrighar's bugs in a pond. Those plate-passing young men on the moon failed to stir me; yet I delight in the infinity of space.

One further comment on my possibly neurotic need for privacy: I've written verse for forty years. All of it has been sent to a remarkable man in Rochester, Dr. James Sibley Watson, who was once the co-owner and deus ex machina of the *Dial* magazine. I have no interest in publication; I simply wish a respected and loved friend to have it all. I've made no effort to persuade publishers to accept my hundreds of non-pop compositions; in fact, even when my kind of pop song was fashionable, I never played half the songs for those Brill Building charmers. I enjoy the act of creating and, much as I love and depend on my friends, I am not impressed by contemporary exposure. What about money? Frankly, it's a miracle I've managed to support myself all these years. My more practical friends are disgusted with my, to them, scatterbrained generosity. For example, I met a remarkable string-bass virtuoso, Gary Karr. He had minimal music to perform, mostly transcriptions. So I wrote him a sonata for bass and piano. I didn't charge him for it or for copying the parts. I was honored that such a talent was interested in having me write something. My friends chided me on the grounds that only he could play the piece. "That's the point," I told them. "I wrote it for him." "But," they snarled, "no one will publish it, etc., etc."

It should be said here that Wilder has never asked for a cent for any of the hundreds of formal pieces he has written. He has done this out of fear that a piece might be rejected, and, more often, simply because he has composed all his formal music voluntarily for people he admires. But this extraordinary largesse has caught up with him. Not long ago, he said, "I've decided to write no more music unless I am paid for it. This is against my most profound convictions. But I'm broke. I know this decision will not bring solvency, as all those who love my free music shall easily be able to do without the boughten stuff. It's very, very sad (for me)."

Which reminds me of my only Hollywood adventure. I was hired for fifteen hundred dollars a week to write the score for a version of "Daddy-Long-Legs." The film was never made, which was too bad, as it was the best score I ever wrote. The lyrics were glorious, by the man who wrote the lyrics for my song "While We're Young" — Bill Engvick.

The producer was also the writer. He sensibly wanted the songs to fit the situations. After we had written over half the songs, he was called away on another film. He told us to sit tight, collect our money, and wait for his return. I refused, on the premise that we wouldn't be earning our salaries. He considered us demented. We came back East and didn't hear from him for three months. At fifteen hundred a week, that would be ugh, ugh . . .

The letters got shorter and more peaceful as they went on. Perhaps Wilder was adjusting to his dental ordeal, or perhaps it was the salubrity of his Cambridge hideout.

ON HIS ABHORRENCE OF POSSESSIONS

Quite a few otherwise friends consider my minimal possessions a quaintness bordering on affectation. My profound need to move constantly, my loathing of leases, and my deep fear of loss I offer to them as adequate reasons for my possessions being limited to the contents of three suitcases. They're seldom convinced. Then I tell them of my Aunt Emma, a most witty and engaging lady whose collecting mania included olive pits. Once, at a funeral, after the coffin had been removed, she wandered from where we sat into the room where the coffin had been. I knew why: to pick up a few scattered flower petals. A salty little man, her brother, called out, "What'cha lookin' for, Em? Olive pits?" Some time later, I was forced to break open one of her many trunks. There, on the top tray, lay about twenty olive pits which had been dipped in gold paint. That could be sufficient reason for limiting my possessions.

Although he detests sentimentality, there is a strong strain of nostalgia in Wilder. But it tends to be a healthy, pastoral nostalgia — the sort that such Romantic poets as William Collins and William Cowper indulged in.

ON HIS DISREGARD FOR THE RECORDED PAST

I've written music for almost fifty years. I've kept no records (or recordings), reviews, interviews, programs, or original sketches of my music. I've kept only a few letters, no books, and have given to others all the presents that were given to me. Indeed, the books I've given away constitute a kind of huge, floating, national library. I have much greater pleasure in recalling an afternoon I spent in Towanda waiting for a westbound Black Diamond (a *real* train with a *real* steam locomotive) than I do a concerto première or a film recording. I remember reading a Thomas Beer novel in a deserted campus somewhere in Maine and the first time I heard Crosby sing "Penthouse Serenade" on a romantic tropical night. In the days when it was rare for a record to reach the million mark,

I had a song on the back of "Paper Doll" which did just that. I was glad to get the ten thousand dollars and indifferent to all the noise about it. When someone enthusiastically tells me he still has my first Octet record, I want to reply, "Have you heard anything I've written since then?," knowing he hasn't.

By the time this letter arrived, Wilder had returned to the Algonquin and was spending most of his evenings at the Cookery, in the Village, where Marian McPartland was appearing. A friend of Wilder's ran into him there one night, and he was startling company. He'd listen intently for minutes, but when the pianist got off a particularly felicitous phrase he'd smite his brow and say in a booming voice, "God *dam*mit! That would have taken me three *weeks* to write, and she does it in three *seconds!*"

ON HIS DISLIKE OF HIRSUTE APPENDAGES

I'm back in the Cookery being distracted by grotesque and Halloween-like hair styles. There's one gray-haired gent (none on his head) who should know better. His sideburns are attached to his mustache by a very narrow bridge of hair, which, in the Cookery's dim light, gives the illusion of the lower part of his face having been shot away. Another fellow, younger, has a perfectly pleasant, even gentle face. But his mustache looks as if it had been drawn on his face with burnt cork while he was sleeping. I keep being told they do no harm with their affectations. I disagree, since they markedly offend my visual need for symmetry. I say "symmetry," but I mean much more. I have found, as has another friend, that we know no man with an affected hair style whom we completely trust or respect. This doesn't apply to young men, though I admit to a constant inner battle required to fight my way past the outer unattractiveness to the face and the self behind the hair.

Wilder's last letter arrived the day before we got together. It was somber but fitting.

ON DEATH

The approach to extinction in my case has caused me to become obsessed with the clarification of all obscurity, sharpening of all dullness, truing of all warp, cutting away all the rot of self-deception, knowing as clearly as I can who and what is doing the dying. I am in a kind of brooding awe of all those who manage to maintain such a powerful self-importance that they truly consider themselves superior beings. Long before I became old, I wept at the sight of death; of all that miraculous energy and affirmation turned to dust. I found myself suddenly against cremation simply because the sight of any but a big city cemetery brought the dead back to a kind of half-life for me. They were not skeletons lying in boxes. They were very faint shadows hovering above their graves. I saw them as the old romantic poets did. So I changed my will from a cadaver gift to a hospital to an old-fashioned corpse to be put in the ground in a box — preferably on a New England hillside. This does not mean that death is my constant companion but that Life, except in its most corrupt and dissolute forms, is a miracle to be all but worshiped. . . . Would the religious need God as much as they do if they comprehended the unique phenomenon of Life?

Wilder said on the telephone that it would be "indecent" to meet in the "riotous confusion" of his hotel room, so we met in a mutual friend's midtown office. Wilder is a tall man with a big head and small feet. He was wearing a sports jacket, gray slacks, and loafers, and they had the resigned look of strictly functional clothes. He has a long, handsome face and receding gray hair that flows out from the back of his head, giving the impression that he is in constant swift motion. His eyebrows are heavy and curved, and when he has finished making a point — often punctuated by his slamming his fist down on the nearest piece of furniture — they shoot up and the corners of his mouth shoot down. He has piercing, deep-set eyes cushioned by dark, doomsday pouches — diamonds resting on velvet. His face is heavily wrinkled — not with the soft, oh-I-am-growing-old lines but with strong, heavy-weather ones. He has a loud baritone voice and he talks rapidly. When he is agitated, his words roll like cannonballs around the room. He laughs a lot and he swears a lot, in an old-fashioned, Mark Twain manner, and when he is seated he leans forward, like a figurehead breasting a flood tide. A small, serene mustache marks the eye of the hurricane.

He smiled brilliantly. "Well, what the dentist did hasn't changed me too much," he said. "And all my friends have been very well-mannered. None have looked away from my mouth and none have stared at it — a bit of subtle eyework for which I'm grateful. I can whistle better than before. In a way, fear and my terrible teeth — those two things — have controlled my life. Somewhere along the line, it was discovered that I'm made largely of glass. I've very little calcium in my bones and none in my teeth. As a result, nothing mends. It's the reason I walk in the hunt-and-peck way I do. I'm in constant fear of banging into something and breaking a leg or falling down

and breaking an arm. I broke my leg in the thirties by jumping off a Fifth Avenue bus on the way to meet my mother,
and I spent six months on my back and six months in a polio
splint. I started out with a bad dentist in Rochester — the kind
who washed his utensils in the kitchen sink and drilled holes
just to have something to fill. When I finally found a good
one, also in Rochester, we had a system whereby I had to go
every three months for a checkup. I'd take him books and think
of jokes to tell him, and I even wrote a piece of music for him,
'A Molar Expedition' — all in hopes that he'd be nice to me.
And once in a while, as a precaution, I'd take his hygienist and
her boy friend out for a drink. Whenever the dentist said
everything was O.K., I'd go out and get drunk. I keep mention-
ing Rochester because I was born there and I still spend a lot
of time there. I was born into a family of bankers. My father
was a banker, my grandfathers were bankers, two uncles were
bankers. They lived that whole ambience of voting Repub-
lican and hating the Jews. They didn't really *hate*, of course.
They just maintained the proper prejudices. My father died
when I was three. My mother didn't know anything about
meat bills and coal bills. She wasn't married until she was
thirty, and she wasn't ready then. She had been a belle who
had been spoiled by her family and by men. She was a Chew,
and she had grown up in a Colonial house surrounded by
English boxwood in the beautiful upstate town of Geneva. It
was a conventional, proper, Henry James life — a safe life,
where there was safe talk and cheerful people and no argu-
ments. The Wilders, on the other hand, were eccentric and
untrammeled. But my mother was a good woman. After she

died, I found a letter in her pocketbook from me saying a string quartet of mine might be performed. But she was embarrassed by my becoming a musician. Musicians were still regarded as servants. When musicians performed at the Eastman house, they came in the side door. I was the youngest of three children. My Edwardian brother lives in New York and can see again, thanks to an eye operation I had to practically force him to undergo. My sister is gone, but I am still indebted to her for singing me early Jerome Kern songs when I was a child. One of them, 'And I'm All Alone,' is still a knock-out. I learned very early that I was perfectly happy to be left alone. So I suppose I became a threat in my own house — an odd boy who was always reading books and who never fought or even played much with other children but who made people laugh. I used the device of foolishness to get by. A while ago, I ran into a childhood friend who has become a self-important tycoon. I used to make him laugh uncontrollably in Rochester. I reminded him of the time we had sneaked into the bishop's house through the milk door and trailed toilet paper all over the place. He didn't even smile. I suppose that is what money does to you. I spent more time with cooks and servants than with anyone else. I even played lousy piano and banjo in an all-black band at a hotel dance in Bay Head, where we went for summers. Since the musicians were all sons of waiters and cooks, it didn't matter my playing with them.

"I went to a couple of private schools in Rochester, and then we moved to Garden City, Long Island, and I was put in St. Paul's School there. I felt *horrible*. So I went to Lawrenceville, and I felt even worse. I finally ran away. Then we moved to Park Avenue — a safe street, of course — and I went to Collegiate.

"A year or so before that, we lived on West Seventieth Street, where, as I recall, I slept in the same bed with my brother. He insisted I whistle 'The Missouri Waltz,' which invariably sent him into a heavy slumber. It does whistle well in thirds. I'd go to a nearby record store to pick up Isham Jones's records, and discovered that the store was near the Sixty-third Street Theater, where Noble Sissle and Eubie Blake's all-black show, *Shuffle Along*, had just opened. I don't remember how many performances I saw, but it was before the carriage trade found the show. The theater was so empty I could slip down to the apron to watch Mr. Blake. It was a revelation. It had the same impact that 'Afternoon of a Faun' had on me. I had thought, until I heard Debussy's piece, that the 'Poet and Peasant Over-ture' was concert music. I went down to *Shuffle Along* to hear all those friendly songs and all those exciting people onstage the way another boy would have hung out at the candy store.

"I graduated from Collegiate, but failed my Regents and never got to Princeton. Instead, I went back to Rochester and studied privately at the Eastman School. I had already started writing music. In fact, the first songs I wrote — for a friend who was giving a show in his family's house at the Jersey shore — were filched from a Princeton Triangle Club show. Nobody caught on until the choral director at Collegiate heard them. The year in New York before I went back to Rochester was a jumble, and largely a lovely one. I spent most of my time with two great friends — Carroll Dunn, whom I'd met in Bay Head, and Lavinia Faxon, now Russ. We talked the nights away in Chinese restaurants, and Lavinia and I still do. I'm going to take her to the Ritz, in Boston, for three days to celebrate her birthday, and I'll have phlox put in her room. I tried, under Carroll's tutelage, to be a writer for a time, and I have a dim recollection of enrolling briefly in a dramatic school. At Eastman, I studied composition and counterpoint with Herbert Inch and with the son of Josiah Royce, the philosopher. I wrote concert songs and a piece for orchestra, and, after hearing Mildred Bailey for the first time over a radio in a speakeasy, I started writing songs for her and Bing Crosby and Ethel Waters. And — by God! — Crosby and Mildred eventually sang them. And at the Eastman I got to know such other students as Mitchell Miller and Goddard Lieberson and John Barrows, the great French horn player, and Jimmy Carroll, as good a clarinetist as ever lived. They were my first professional friends. They made it possible for me to stop sidling in my shyness down the halls of Eastman."

I ordered up a large coffee and a piece of pound cake from Schrafft's for Wilder. He put out his cigarette and immediately lit another one. He stared moodily into space, and for an instant he looked like that famous brooding photograph of Eugene O'Neill. "I've always been a great coffee drinker, but I'm an even greater one since I quit the booze. A succession of trivia finally made me stop. One day, bowed down by a *monstrous* hangover, I successively lost in twenty minutes my wallet, which had five hundred and forty dollars in it that I had saved for a trip, broke a pair of glasses, and stepped on my favorite pipe. That did it. My drinking never stopped me from working, but it made me a lot of enemies. I was one of those deceptive drinkers who don't show their condition. I invariably got venomous and nasty and rude when I was drunk, but I didn't *look* drunk. On top of that, I never remembered a thing the next day, so it was very difficult to apologize adequately when some kind friend called and recounted my atrocities. But I'll say one thing: I never once bought a bottle and holed up in my hotel room. I did *all* my drinking in bars. I guess I started in earnest in the late twenties. I had begun voyaging back and forth between Rochester and New York, and I was writing a lot of popular music. Most of it is on file up at Bill Engvick's house, on the Hudson. I keep meaning to go up there and look at it, but I never seem to. Then, in the late thirties, partly at the behest of Mitchell Miller and partly because of the late Morty Palitz, an A. and R. man and songwriter, I wrote my first woodwind octet pieces. I had been fooling around with the harpsichord, and of course Mitchell was an oboist. So I added a clarinet, a flute, a bass clarinet, a bassoon, a string bass, and drums, and we made some records for Columbia. It must have been around nineteen thirty-eight. I gave the pieces nutty titles, like 'A Debutante's Diary,' 'Sea Fugue Mama,' 'Neurotic Goldfish,' 'The House Detective Registers,' 'The Children Met the Train,' and 'Jack, This Is My Husband.' As afterthoughts. The pieces were not program music. When the records came out, they were gunned down by the jazz boys because they had a classical flavor and they were gunned down by the classical boys because they had a jazz flavor. Now, I'm told, they are beginning to be thought of seriously, and there is even talk they may be reissued. Ha! Anyway, I kept my head above water

by writing arrangements for the big bands and by arranging
songs for people like Frank Sinatra and Mildred Bailey. I
was hip-deep in the pop music world, and I *hated* it. In the
mid-forties, I wrote my first and probably last song hits, and
then, in the early fifties, a marvelous thing happened. John
Barrows arrived in New York, and I started writing chamber
music. He believed in me, and that was all I needed.

"Well, I've got to head back to the Algonquin. I told Marian
McPartland I'd stop in tonight with a new piano piece, and
I still have to finish it. Come back with me, and I'll buy you
a drink at the hotel." It was a seven- or eight-block walk down
Fifth Avenue to Forty-fourth Street, and at least once a block
Wilder, who talked the whole way, interrupted himself to
make judicious comments about the passing hair styles and
about another fond aversion — the new-style clown-sized bow
ties. He walked advisedly, as if each pedestrian represented
a potential fracture or contusion. "I prefer slightly seedy sur-
roundings to work in," he said. "Then I'm forced to create a
little loveliness. I've worked all over the country — in Chicago
and San Francisco, at the University of Wisconsin, in a big
room full of Chinese porcelain just off Brattle Street, in Cambridge, in a hotel in Brunswick, Georgia, and Abingdon, Vir-
ginia, in Key West, in a studio at the Eastman School, upstairs
at the Algonquin, in my publisher's office, on Columbus Circle.
I can't work in Los Angeles and I can't work in Maine. Maine
is my Achilles' heel. I go there and slough off everything. I
go there without guilt. I let Maine take over — the smell of
the kelp, the rocks, the bayberry leaves, the fogs, the tides,
that marvelous relationship between the land and the sea. I

work in terrific spurts. I've written a four- or five-movement piece in three weeks. One year, I wrote twelve long pieces. I try and keep myself where I'm just finishing up one piece and starting another. I do this because I'm terrified of the dry spells I occasionally have. I had one six months ago in Rochester in the little hotel I stay in there, and it was a beaut. When it used to happen, I'd go out and drink, but now I read. In Rochester, I even went to the library and took out a thesis analyzing my music. I read it to try and find out how I write, but it didn't do any good. I couldn't even understand what the writer was talking about. I'll be going back to Rochester soon, though, because the University of Rochester is giving me an honorary degree." Wilder's initial, horrified reaction to the news of the honorary degree was that he would tell the university he could not possibly accept, because he would be on an essential business trip in Liechtenstein at the time. He finally accepted, but immediately afterward gave the citation to a friend for safekeeping. "I work almost wholly intuitively. I have a few little technical things I use, but I believe that technique is a composer's secret; any composer who talks about technique is simply offering a substitute for content. I have an innate sense of order, balance, and shape. I know most of the rules of counterpoint, although I never studied theory. When I start a piece, I try and find a melodic idea that I consider seminal, that I think will hold up. Then I find secondary themes as I move along. I work at the piano more often than not. I will play the parts I've written very slowly, and I'll work as hard on eight sixteenth notes, trying to get that right balance and flow and feeling, as I will on an entire piece. It's a process of searching and searching. Once in a while, I'll finish a passage where I *know* something is wrong. So I'll look and look until I've found the trouble and made it *right*. There was a time, years ago, when I'd get clever and simply skirt the trouble by throwing up a persiflage of counter-notes or a fancy rhythmic turn, but it never worked. The performer would spot it the second or third time through, and I'd get scolded. I still have technical gaps. A while back, I had to ask John Barrows what a passacaglia is. It turned out I had used one in a piece I'd done for him and didn't know it. Then he told me that as a child his mother had played a certain Bach piece for him, and that it shocked him. He didn't understand it. Twenty years later, his musical training finished, he went back to the piece and found that all his schooling didn't make the piece any easier for him, even though he now understood the complex musical and intellectual games Bach was playing in it. I love the act of composing, but when I finish a piece that's it. I don't really care if it's performed; I can't stand listening to many of my pieces more than once. I put the piece out of my mind. If I'm told it's not good, I'm not shattered because I'm already free of it. If I'm told it *is* good, I don't pay any attention. Self-adulation would just get in my way. So it's a clearing-house process in which I make continual room for new things. If I was protective of my work, storing it all up in my head, I'd probably stop writing. I'd be too busy contemplating my navel. Players tend to like what I write; composers don't. Composers think of performers as necessary evils, and it's the same with playwrights and actors. But I consider the written music only a guide. The notes sug*gest*, they tell only part of the story.

I'll take half the credit, and all the rest goes to the performer. Performers! Those great, beautiful people are my saviors.

"People have often compared composing and improvising, saying that composition is improvisation in slow motion and that improvisation is instant composition. Well! Composing is a slow, arduous, obvious, inch by inch process, whereas improvisation is a lightning mystery. In fact, it's *the* creative mystery of our age, and I wonder how many people know that. I wish to God that some neurologists would sit down and figure out *how* the improviser's brain works, *how* he selects, out of hundreds of thousands of possibilities, the notes he does and at the speed he does — *how*, in God's name, his mind works so damned fast! And why, when the notes come out right, they *are* right. Maybe we'll just have to go on thinking of it on the folk level as a series of secrets paraded in public. Musicians *talk* to one another when they improvise, and they say things they wouldn't *dare* say in words. It's all a terrific act of confession."

We turned in to the Algonquin, and it was as if the squire were returning to his country house at the end of the London season. Wilder, smiling and bowing his head, called the doorman and the bellmen by name, greeted the people behind the desk, and, after saying hello to a waiter and inquiring about his cold, selected a table in a far corner of the nearly empty lobby. He ordered a cup of coffee for himself and a vodka and tonic for me. "This place is the nearest thing I have to a home," he said, leaning back in his chair and surveying his domain. "I've been coming here since I was a child, and there are still people on the staff who have been here almost as long as I have. They take care of me. They send out my laundry without my having to fill out a laundry slip, they hang a few suits for me when I'm away, they forward my mail, and they shepherded me through my drinking days. I sat here once with someone I couldn't abide — I think he had something to do with my family — and I had sixteen Martinis. He was a big drinker, and I thought I'd show him and be an even bigger one. I got in a cab to go uptown to a restaurant, and when I got there I simply couldn't *move*. I told the driver to take me back to the Algonquin, and whoever was on the door sized up the situation immediately. A bellman appeared, and he and the doorman made one of those four-handed seats, got me onto it, and whisked me up to my room. But the important thing is I can be packed and out of my room in twenty minutes. *That* is the breath of life for me, and I guess it's one of the reasons I never got married. My sort of life completely denies the female nest-building instinct. Another reason is my terrific sense of responsibility. If I *had* gotten married — and the wedding bells *were* about to ring for me several times — I would have had a fireman, a policeman, and a doctor living in at all times. I would have worried endlessly about the house burning down, about the babies being mongoloid, about the furniture getting scratched, about the wife getting a cold. And another reason is that I don't think most women can stand music. It's too amorphous."

Wilder took a sip of coffee and looked a little apprehensive. It was four-thirty, and the lobby was beginning to fill up. "Years ago, I'd check out when I had a little money and get on a train, and I'd stay on trains for weeks at a time. I'd travel the main trunks, and I'd transfer and take all the spur lines. I loved sitting in a junction in the back of the beyond on a hot day and reading a long novel and listening to the chatter between the baggage man and the conductor. I loved talking with the engineer when he oiled his engine." Wilder barked and slapped his brow. "Can you imagine nattering with a man refueling a jet? I remember coming down from Crawford Notch, in New Hampshire, and the train making meal stops. There would be a big M on the timetable, and everybody would get off and eat — either a full meal in the station restaurant, which was very good, or homemade sandwiches sold by a local lady. So my life has been divided between travel and music and my friends and solitude. Occasionally I just lock my door and stay alone, and that way I can refill my cup. Then, when I open the door and take off again, I have something to pass along. I hate to see people I love unless I have enough to give them."